BRIGHT NOTES

THE POETRY OF JOHN DRYDEN

Intelligent Education

Nashville, Tennessee

BRIGHT NOTES: The Poetry of John Dryden
www.BrightNotes.com

No part of this publication may be used or reproduced in any manner whatsoever without written permission, except in the case of brief quotations in critical articles and reviews. For permissions, contact Influence Publishers http://www.influencepublishers.com.

ISBN: 978-1-645424-64-2 (Paperback)
ISBN: 978-1-645424-65-9 (eBook)

Published in accordance with the U.S. Copyright Office Orphan Works and Mass Digitization report of the register of copyrights, June 2015.

Originally published by Monarch Press.
Christopher Russell Reaske, 1965
2020 Edition published by Influence Publishers.

Interior design by Lapiz Digital Services. Cover Design by Thinkpen Designs.

Printed in the United States of America.

Library of Congress Cataloging-in-Publication Data forthcoming.
Names: Intelligent Education
Title: BRIGHT NOTES: The Poetry of John Dryden
Subject: STU004000 STUDY AIDS / Book Notes

CONTENTS

1) Introduction to John Dryden — 1

2) Early Poems — 20

3) Annus Mirabilis — 32

4) The Satires — 52

5) Verse Essays — 94

6) Odes — 138

7) Critical Commentary — 151

8) Bibliography — 160

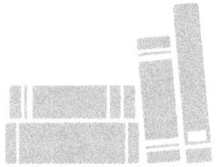

INTRODUCTION TO JOHN DRYDEN

BIOGRAPHY OF DRYDEN

Early Background

John Dryden was born in Aldwinkle, Northamptonshire on August 9, 1631, the year that John Milton reached the age of twenty-three. Dryden's family was of Cumberland stock, although it had already been firmly entrenched in Northamptonshire for several generations. The roots of Dryden's family were consistently Puritan and anti-monarchial: The Pickerings - the family of Dryden's mother - were rigorous supporters of Cromwell; Sir Erasmus Dryden chose prison rather than give financial assistance to King Charles I.

At Westminister School

Dryden was admitted to the Westminister School where he became a "king's scholar" and studied under the direction of the now-famous headmaster, Dr. Busby. At Westminister Dryden wrote a few satires, made a prize translation of Persius, a Latin poet, and wrote the famous elegiac verses on the death of his school friend Henry, Lord Hastings. This three-fold combination of **satire**, translation, and poetry demonstrated a pattern of versatility that was to carry Dryden through numerous financial hardship. It is also interesting to note that the famous English philosopher John Locke was at Westminister when Dryden was there.

At Trinity College, Cambridge

In May of 1650, exactly one decade prior to the restoration of Charles II to the English throne, Dryden entered Trinity College, Cambridge. About Dryden's career at Cambridge, relatively little is known. The only incident recorded is that Dryden appears to have been punished for two weeks for having disobeyed the Vice Master. One thing, however, is certain: at Cambridge Dryden began to write with more discipline and energy. He published a poem written to his friend John Hoddeson in 1650; in 1653 he wrote a love-letter, a curious blending of prose and **rhyme**, to his cousin Honor Dryden, an eighteen-year-old girl. Some critics speculate about the relationship between Dryden and his cousin; Honor never married, which has been interpreted as proof that she was in love with Dryden.

Dryden's father died in June, 1654, leaving his twenty-three-year-old son, who had graduated with a B.A. degree in January of the same year, an income of about fifty pounds a month. As the eldest of the family's fourteen children, it was appropriate that Dryden receive the inheritance.

The next three years in Dryden's life form one of those gaps which are often found in the biographies of famous poets. It is possible that he simply stayed on at Cambridge. In any case, the three years that are unaccounted for may well have been devoted to study, for Dryden's first major poem displays sound scholarly discipline and a complete familiarity with scholarly matter.

Off To London

Biographers seem to agree that in the middle of 1657, Dryden went to live in London, where he became a secretary, or clerk, in the Cromwellian Commonwealth Government. It is probable that he was either hired by or working for his cousin, Sir Gilbert Pickering, Cromwell's Lord Chamberlain, who had been summoned to Cromwell's House of Lords in the same year.

In 1658, several days after the death and burial of Cromwell, Dryden eulogized Cromwell in a long group of elegiac "Heroic Stanzas: Consecrated to the Glorious Memory of His Most Serene and Renown'd Highness, Oliver, Late Lord Protector of This Commonwealth, and Co." About this time, Dryden went to live at the home of his first publisher, Herringman, with whom Dryden did business until 1679. (In that year, Jacob Tonson became his publisher.) In any case, it is important to remember that it was immediately upon the publication of his "Heroic Stanzas" on Cromwell that Dryden became famous as a poet.

Dryden's Opportunism

There are a great many unpleasant things which can be said about Dryden, and one is that he was an opportunist and a compromiser. In 1660, it was not difficult for a young man in his twenties of meager financial means, to transfer his loyalties from the deceased Cromwell to the living king, Charles II. In several poems devoted to the restoration of Charles II, notably in *Astraea Redux*, "A Poem On The Happy Restoration and Return of His Sacred Majesty Charles the Second," (1660) and in "A Panegyric on his Coronation," Dryden boisterously and enthusiastically endorsed the new king.

Those who criticize Dryden's change of sympathies should bear in mind that most of England underwent a change of heart as well. But if it is any compensation, *Astraea Redux* is an inferior poem compared to the earlier, Puritan Dryden's "Heroic Stanzas."

In any case, Dryden's change of affection did not alienate him from any of his contemporaries. This was the age of patronage; aspiring poets dedicated their poems to, or wrote them about people in a position to help the poet's career. The king had great power to place behind a poet, as did most wealthy members of the upper class and the aristocracy. During the period of 1660 to 1662, Dryden also wrote poems addressed to Sir Robert Howard, who was to become his brother-in-law, and to Dr. Charleton, upon whose recommendation Dryden was elected to the Royal Society.

Dryden's Marriage

Dryden had become a friend of the Earl of Berkshire and the father of Lady Elizabeth Howard, sister of Robert. On December 1, 1663, Dryden married Elizabeth. The marriage is generally believed to have been unpleasant. Dryden, at thirty-two, was considerably younger than his wife, who had a reputation for moral looseness. But aside from bearing him three children, Dryden's wife brought him financial and social elevation. By the time Dryden was forty, he was in a position to lend the king 500 pounds as an investment.

Dryden The Dramatist

With the Restoration reopening of the theaters that Cromwell had previously ordered closed, Dryden, eager for financial gain, determined to become a dramatist. He felt that his own natural inclination lay toward tragedy, and during the first year of the Restoration, he wrote a tragedy on Henry, Duke of Guise. However, friends convinced him not to allow it to be performed.

Feeling disinclined to write another tragedy, Dryden decided to try his hand at comedy. He realized that in so doing he was writing for the public rather than for himself, for as he wrote in an essay: "I confess my chief endeavors are to delight the age in which I live. If the humor of this be for low comedy, small accidents and raillery, I will force my genius to obey it, though with more reputation I could write in verse. I know I am not so fitted by nature to write comedy; I want that quality of humor which is required to it. My conversation is slow and dull; my humor saturnine and reserved; in short, I am none of those who endeavor to break jests in company or makes repartees." In short, Dryden realized that the Restoration theater audiences wanted low comedy, and that is what he proceeded to write.

His first attempt to meet this public demand was a prose comedy, *The Wild Gallant*. Performed in February 1663, it was an immediate failure. As the diarist of the age - Samuel Pepys - wrote: Dryden's play was "so poor a thing as ever I saw in my life." Based on a Spanish story, the play was designed to satisfy the audience's love of wit and immorality, but it had none of the charm of the Restoration dramas of Etherege or Congreve. The same is unfortunately true of Dryden's other comedies. But *The Rival Ladies*, his second comedy, was better than his first and earned from Pepys the description of "a very innocent and most pretty witty play." Dryden's comedies have an extravagance that he never was able to control or diminish. Much of the rowdy, immoral humor has the tenor of a naive schoolboy telling a dirty joke. But we must bear in mind that Dryden knew perfectly well that he was not gifted for writing comedy, and his career as a comic dramatist comprises a relatively minor part of his life as a practicing poet.

Success

Success in the theater finally came to Dryden with *The Indian Queen*, a tragedy in heroic verse, on which his brother-in-law, Sir Robert Howard, had collaborated. This play was so successful that Dryden committed himself to writing heroic verse from then on. These "heroic plays" were written in "heroic couplets" in iambic **pentameter**. In this style Dryden was to write about one play a year for nineteen years. The list of his produced plays is formidable numbering such tragedies as *Secret Love*, *Tyrannic Love*, *Amboyna*, and *The Conquest of Granada*. Almost all of Dryden's plays were filled with songs, and sixty of these were popular enough to merit incorporation into late seventeenth-century songbooks. But the heroic plays did not only have songs; they also had panegyrics, prologues, epilogues, and prefaces, many of which were printed separately.

During the middle part of the century, there was a renewed interest in Shakespeare. Dryden consequently "adapted" Shakespeare's *Troilus and Cressida*, and based his *All For Love* on Shakespeare's *Antony and Cleopatra*. It was typical of Dryden to ride the wave of the popular style.

In summary, Dryden had a long and experimental career as a playwright. From the first reopening of the theaters in 1660, until November 1681 (the year that Dryden wrote the famous *Absalom and Achitophel*), Dryden wrote almost nothing but plays. These dramas still comprise the bulk of his literary output, but it was not until he turned to writing his great satirical poems that his full power as poet was felt. Until that time, the stage was Dryden's main source of income and his own way of meeting the age's demand for low comedy and tragic drama.

Turning To Satire

In 1679, when Dryden was forty-eight, he was insulted by a contemporary dramatist, Thomas Shadwell. Shadwell thought little of Dryden's plays and publicly praised *The Rehearsal*, a drama written by George Villiers, which openly mocked both Dryden the man and Dryden the dramatist. Dryden fought back by writing the first of his famous verse satires, Mac Flecknoe, in which Dryden energetically attacked Shadwell and made him the inheritor of the dullness of a deceased minor poet, Richard Flecknoe. Although written in 1679, Mac Flecknoe circulated only in private until 1683, when it was finally published anonymously in an unauthorized edition.

Dryden's reputation as a satirist grew rapidly. In 1674 Dryden's friend, the Earl of Mulgrave, wrote "An Essay on Satire," attacking the Earl of Rochester and two of the king's mistresses; however, because of Dryden's reputation as a satirist, he was believed to be the author and was therefore beaten by hired thugs in Rose Alley, Covent Garden.

Against A "Popish Plot"

Three years later (in 1681) Dryden took up his satirical pen once again. A "popish plot" - to create fear of Catholic domination in England - was in the making. The leader of the troublemakers, a Whig named the Earl of Shaftesbury was advocating that King Charles' illegitimate son, the Duke of Monmouth, a Protestant, should be the successor to the throne, rather than the intended successor, James, Charles' Catholic brother.

The Whig-inspired propaganda was effective: fearing another Catholic ruler, England drifted toward civil war. Dryden found a Biblical parallel to the situation in the Old Testament story of *Absalom and Achitophel*. Dryden's master **satire** of this name mirrored effectively the characters and the atmosphere of the Whig dissatisfaction and rebellion. Considered today one of the most brilliant **satires** in the English language, *Absalom and Achitophel* went through nine editions in two years during its own time.

When Shaftesbury was acquitted of the charge of high treason in 1682, the Whigs struck a medal to commemorate the event. Dryden slashed out vehemently with the highly invective **satire**, *The Medal*. This was followed the same year by "The Second Part of *Absalom and Achitophel*." However, Dryden wrote only two hundred of the thousand-odd lines; the rest was written by his contemporary, Nahum Tate. In the same year, Dryden's *Mac Flecknoe* was published for the first time, and *Religio Laici*, an attack on the Papists, established Dryden as the acknowledged master of verse satire.

Dryden's Conversion To Catholicism

James II, a Catholic, acceded to the throne in 1685. In the same year Dryden converted to Catholicism. As with his earlier shift of loyalty from Cromwell to Charles II, Dryden's action appears opportunistic. There has been endless debate over whether Dryden's conversion was sincere. Some have argued that Dryden's wife, after all, had been a Roman Catholic for several years, and his son had converted while at Cambridge. But we cannot help but wonder why Dryden's conversion took place in the same year as the accession of James II. Dryden made an elaborate defense of his conversion and of Roman Catholicism in general in his 1687 *The Hind and The Panther*. After this poem was published, Dryden performed various literary services for the king, including a savage attack on Stilling fleet, who had criticized two papers published by King James unfavorably.

Revolution

But after the revolution rejecting James II, and the subsequent accession of William and Mary, Dryden did not renounce Catholicism. In light of this he deserves credit, and for this the criticism of his earlier changes of loyalty is usually softened. In any case, his refusal to give up his Catholicism when the Country had rejected a Catholic king resulted in his financial and social alienation. At fifty-eight, Dryden suddenly found himself in a state of actual and social poverty.

The Last Years

In Order to survive, Dryden attempted - successfully - to exist on his writing alone, thus establishing himself as England's first professional author. He wrote some spurious plays; "tagged" (set to **rhyme**) Milton's *Paradise Lost* - the result was the weak *The State of Innocence and Fall of Man*; and made a series of translations, including five **satires** of the Roman satirist, Juvenal, Ovid's Amores and Ars Amatoria, and a complete Virgil, which was so popular it earned him some twelve hundred pounds. In the year before his death, at the age of sixty-nine, Dryden produced his *Fables, Ancient and Modern*, a collection of stories taken primarily from Boccaccio and Chaucer. His last work, *The*

Secular Masque, was relatively unimportant, but is interesting for its reflection of the atmosphere of the age in which he had lived.

In his last year, the aging poet was visited by Addison, Congreve, and Dryden's disciple, Alexander Pope. Dryden died on May 1, 1700 at his home on Gerrard Street in London.

Dryden's Prose

Dryden's writing life was busy and varied. The dramas were preparation for the poetry which later established his reputation. But Dryden the dramatist and Dryden the poet were also in the company of Dryden, the writer of prose.

"Dryden," Dr. Johnson wrote in his *Life of Dryden*, "may be properly considered as the father of English criticism, as the writer who first taught us to determine upon principles the merit of composition...Dryden's *Essay On Dramatic Poetry* was the first regular and valuable treatise on the art of writing."

Dryden's *Essay On Dramatic Poetry* (1668) was his first important prose work, and it established him as an important literary critic. It takes the form of a dialogue between several characters representative of different theories about drama, in which Dryden, as the character Neander, argues that English drama is better than the French, and that it also does not need the model of classical drama; the essay also contains a famous critique of Ben Jonson's play, *The Silent Woman*.

The bulk of Dryden's prose criticism was published in the form of prefaces and dedications, which he affixed to his plays.

He defended his essay on dramatic poetry, for example, in a preface to a second edition of his play, *The Indian Emperor* (1668). Dryden's prose style is remarkably clear and concise. Only as he grew older did he begin to write complexly structured sentences. Dryden's final piece of critical writing, the preface to the *Fables*, is in a relaxed informal style which became a model for later English prose essayists.

INTELLECTUAL CLIMATE OF THE AGE

The Restoration

Dryden's age was one of flux in all areas, but none was more turbulent than the political arena of change and rebellion. Nothing had a greater effect on Dryden - and the Country as a whole - than the changes in the ruler of England. The Puritan Commonwealth Government had depended entirely on the peculiar genius of Oliver Cromwell. Thus, in 1660, less than two years after Cromwell's death, Charles II was able to return from exile to "restore" Stuart leadership in England.

The idea of "Restoration" describes most of the phenomena and underlines most of the problems of the century. Most of England was ecstatic to have Charles II back again, but there of course remained an oppositionist group of Puritans.

Charles' successor, his brother James, was also a Catholic, but James' harsh, intolerant treatment of the Protestants finally led England to rebel against Catholic domination and to invite William and Mary to assume the throne. This event, known as the "Glorious Revolution," was accomplished in 1688 by the English Parliament, rather than by invocation of the "divine law." England had expected tolerance with the return of Charles II, but the Country had been unpleasantly surprised. As a result, England gradually drifted away from Catholic leadership.

Moral Laxity Of The Restoration

When the brief era of Puritan leadership came to an end, it was perhaps inevitable that England would react against the severe Puritan morality. Many English cavaliers who had been living in exile in France now returned to England, equipped with a racy, more sophisticated attitude that hastened England into an era of loose living. King Charles II himself was no exception, and his court was characterized by hedonism and a self-indulgent morality; the Puritan ethos was completely inverted. The Restoration drama reflected this new attitude toward moral behavior: court wit became stage wit. Many amateurs entered the explosively popular field of drama from the court; among the major court wits who reigned in dramatic circles (from about 1665 to 1680) were George Villiers, the Duke of Buckingham; Charles Sackville; Lord Buckhurst; Sir Charles Sedley; and the top ranking John Wilmot, the Earl of Rochester (1647-80) Wilmot's dramas were extremely popular and are frequently cited as examples of Restoration theater.

A New Urbanity

Restoration comedy focused primarily on the life of the city; most of the new, loose values were amply displayed in London. The city provided a rich source of variegated material for the stage. We must not forget that Cromwell had closed the theaters in 1642; as the theater had been shut up for eighteen years, it is neither surprising nor horrible that England's theater-goers suddenly demanded the most lively and least moral kind of theater that could be presented. The new stage hedonism was thus little more than a massive reaction to the stern Puritan ethics.

The New Wit

It cannot be too strongly emphasized that in the time following the 1660 Restoration, London demanded wit. No poet or dramatist could survive without a keen sense of it. It has been said that Dryden's wit, for example, was so sharp it could sever an enemy's head from his body without leaving a mark - it was not, in other words, a bludgeoning or naive kind. This was an age that quite literally elevated intellect above imagination. Both drama and poetry were characterized by their intellectual mockery of the old Puritan system of values; there are countless witty attacks on marriage, virtue, and sobriety.

John Dryden, as Louis Untermeyer has noted, symbolized this age, sometimes known as The Age of Reason. Dryden was, typically, a servant of the current status quo and could change his loyalties without attracting much criticism. This was an age that realized that survival depended on a willingness to compromise - whether with regard to politics, religion, or literature. Dryden, as typical of his age, was perfectly willing to forego idealistic and perhaps unattainable goals for concrete, less idealistic, attainable ones. Dryden was a practical man who used his head rather than his emotions as his guide. As a man of formidable intellectual prowess, Dryden used his mind for his own personal gain, and in so doing, his personality came to symbolize the times.

One cannot help but contrast Dryden with Milton, whose *Paradise Lost* was published in 1667, just eight months prior to Dryden's appointment as Poet Laureate of England. Milton's life was spent in the midst of religious and political struggle; his entire middle years were devoted to ecclesiastical and civil problems. But Dryden, whose middle years were no less surrounded by various kinds of strife, chose to accommodate change and to serve the party in power.

Religion

In the age of Dryden, there were three distinct forms of the Christian religion: the Establishment, or English Anglican Church; that of the Puritan dissenters; and Catholicism. There was not only disagreement and friction among these three factions; there was struggle within each of the three. At the same time, all three were in continuous competition with the philosophic skepticism which challenged the usefulness of all kinds of knowledge - and Christian scripture as well. Throughout the sixteenth and seventeenth centuries, a reaction against the fundamentally rationalistic outlook of the middle ages was being introduced, both on the Continent and in England.

After the Restoration of 1660, the Anglican Establishment comprised most of the Nation; the Protestant dissenters were mostly men of the commercial class of London; the Roman Catholics were no more than a tiny minority. The Anglicans combined the Bible and tradition to form the basis of their belief; the dissenters wanted the exclusive use of the Bible; and the Catholics wanted the exclusive use of the tradition of Church interpretation. Politically, the Anglicans were in favor of a monarchy; the dissenters were for parliament and against monarchy; and the Catholics were accused of trying to make England subservient to France. Thus in both politics and religion, Dryden's age was filled with chaos: in all areas, England was undergoing radical change. Scientific discoveries opened up new areas of learning, while at the same time, skeptics battered at the very idea of learning. The map of the world was being changed by the series of discoveries of its explorers, while the map of England's emotional state was repeatedly altered with a series of changes in leadership. As Lord Macaulay wrote, "Of Dryden...it may be said that the course which he pursued, and the effect which he produced, depended less on his personal qualities than on the circumstances in which he was placed...it is the age that forms the man, not the man that forms the age."

New Attitude Toward Poetry

The movement from the Elizabethan to the Augustan Age constitutes one of the greatest leaps in the history of English literature. In the late 1600's, there developed a completely new attitude toward poetry, which would assert an influence on the direction English poetry would take for the next century. In brief, the new attitude elevated the idea of "decorum," or fitness of poetic language; that is, it made language part of the criterion for evaluating a poem. The new attitude also placed a new emphasis on urbanity, wit, and elegance - all of which are well illustrated by Dryden. **Satire** and wit replaced the classicism and allusion of Milton.

DRYDEN'S STYLE

The Heroic Style

Most of Dryden's poetry is written in "heroic style." The voice we hear in *Annus Mirabilis*, in the heroic plays, and in *Absalom and Achitophel*, for example, speaks in an heroic, or lofty and serious manner - as it does in most of Dryden's "celebrating poems." To write in this lofty style, it was essential that Dryden's language have seriousness, dignity, and a general sense of formality. Whenever he was celebrating a public occasion, Dryden carefully selected measured rhythms and an elevated, serious language. This style was further heightened by frequent classical and Biblical allusions.

We must of course realize that in choosing this heroic, grand kind of poetry, Dryden was satisfying the age's expectations of a "Poet Laureate," the official position which Dryden held from 1670 to 1689. On the other hand, we cannot explain Dryden's heightened seriousness and heroic use of language only in this way, for Dryden wrote in a similar style both before and after he was made **Poet Laureate**. Perhaps the award of this public office sharpened Dryden's latent inclination toward the solemn, heroic style. Most of Dryden's poetry, after all, was public, and usually commemorated some national event or public figure. His major poems deal with events or personalities: the 1659 "Heroic Stanzas" on Cromwell; *Aestraea Redux* on Charles II; *Annus Mirabilis* addressed to London; Threnodia Augustalis on the death of Charles II. Dryden's poetry therefore has little of the private, emotional utterance so common (and now apparently necessary) to twentieth-century poetry. This does not mean, of course, that Dryden was insincere. Some of his commendatory poems express ideas which Dryden held privately for many years. Dryden merely felt that a poet should concentrate on subjects aside from himself; as he wrote, "Anything, though ever so little which a man speaks of himself, in my opinion is still too much."

Rhetorical Devices

Dryden achieves an elevated style by using most of the possible standard rhetorical devices. Among them are hyperbole, repetition, personification, apostrophe, exclamation, questioning, balance, and inversion. The tone is further elevated by the classical and Biblical **allusions** which had already been so richly exploited in the poetry of Milton. Through the employment of these rhetorical skills, Dryden's style obtains a sense of grandeur, particularly in his panegyrics.

As several critics have shown, part of Dryden's poetic power lies in his use of one of the greatest rhetorical devices, forensic skill. While the content, or subject matter, of many of the debates in Dryden's poetry is of questionable taste, the fact remains that the debates are carried out in highly skillful manner. Dryden had a great capacity for oratory, and this capacity was continuously sharpened as he carried out the many speaking engagements that went with the job of **Poet Laureate**. (He had to give many commencement addresses, for example.) Dryden's oratory blended well with argument. Dryden considered it to be the dramatist's duty to overpower the audience, to bring the spectators into submission: that is, the dramatist, through the speeches of his characters, should exert a persuasive influence over the audience. This habit of mind is strongly illustrated by the debates which Dryden presents: he "defends" the Roman Catholic Church in *The Hind and The Panther*, while he is both prosecutor and defender in *Absalom and Achitophel*. Another example is the magnificent use of debate in his famous prose essay on dramatic poetry. Debate, in short, is one of the central features of Dryden's poetry.

Dryden's Classicism

Dryden was in the neo-classical tradition of late English Renaissance literature. That is, he was thoroughly acquainted with the ancient classics and could allude to them easily. Dryden was able to imitate the **epic** style, but unlike Milton, Dryden used it to heighten his **satire**. He wrote in what has been called a "mock-epic" or "mock-heroic" style which parodied and underscored much of the sincere expression of classical **epic**. (Alexander Pope copied Dryden's mock-heroic style in poems like the *Dunciad*, and *The Rape of The Lock*.) Much of Dryden' **allusion** has been shown to function ironically. (See the article by R. A. Brower in the Bibliography.) Dryden worked diligently to discover relevant parallels between ancient and modern situations and made the present (or a personality of the present) seem dull or foolish by contrast with the past. Dryden's **allusions** are thus often filled with a keen sense of humor and form an intrinsic part of his satiric mode.

The Poetic Whole

In contrast to Milton's poetry, the poetry of Dryden does not easily lend itself to passage analysis. We do not usually think of long, brilliant passages in Dryden, for the main unit of Dryden's poetry is the single line. Many popular quotations from Dryden are no more than one line, for the reason that Dryden is frequently only good for one line - not for several in a row, and certainly not for a sustained period of time. But even more graphically than in the single line, Dryden's poetic gift is displayed in the "poetic whole." That is, Dryden skillfully directs the audience's attention to a single, main subject of interest. There is little discursive wandering or digression in Dryden's poetry. Dryden sometimes pursues a single **metaphor** throughout a work, and sometimes this pursuit is presented in the form of an allegory - as in *The Hind and The Panther*, and in *Absalom and Achitophel*. Dryden's poetic skill, in other words, is most easily seen in his sustained discussion of a single topic: sometimes carried out by way of a rhetorical debate, and sometimes by way of pervasive, large **metaphors** which defy disunity.

Union Of Style With Scope Of Learning

One of the critical problems encountered in approaching the poetry of Dryden is that of trying to reconcile a seemingly unimaginative mind with an extremely imaginative poetic craftsman. It has generally been argued that Dryden was primarily a poet in the technical sense and only secondarily a poet in the intellectual sense. Dryden's "expression," in other words, is usually considered more impressive than his "thought." Such an inequality, if true, would constitute a serious problem for any poet.

Both Dr. Johnson and T. S. Eliot were attracted to Dryden's verbal dexterity. It is undeniably true that Dryden's skill with handling words and in using words in new ways was formidable. There is little doubt, furthermore, that Dryden sincerely wanted to improve the flexibility of the English language. However, Dryden wanted to perfect his tools only in order to perfect his product. It is wrong to divorce his broad scope of learning from his equally broad experimentation with stylistic changes. It would be relatively fruitless to approach Dryden as only a craftsman and not as a thinker. There is a balance between his broad reading and his rhetorical flourish, and we must search for the mainspring of that balance as we read through his poetry.

EARLY POEMS

"UPON THE DEATH OF LORD HASTINGS"

Introduction

This poem, Dryden's first published work, was one of a collection of poems written in the memory of Henry, Lord Hastings, a nineteen-year-old school friend of Dryden who died of smallpox in 1649. Marvell, Herrick, Denham, Waller, and Brome also wrote poems for the small volume, which also contained Dryden's first poem, Lachrymae Musarum. The book was published in the same year. By topic, but not by style, Dryden's poem is similar to the young Milton's **elegy** Lycidas, which is also a poem mourning the death of a school friend.

SUMMARY

Lines 1-38

Dryden uses a conventional elegiac opening by commenting on the apparent injustice implied by the premature death of a gifted young man. Dryden questions God's justice by wondering why someone as virtuous as Henry should have been rushed to so early a death. Why should one bother to be virtuous, or pursue art, if death will end all, too soon. Dryden again follows the **conventions** of **elegy** as he shifts to a praise of the deceased friend's linguistic abilities; Hastings, a very learned student, was so skilled in languages that "His native soil was the four parts o' th'earth" (line 21). Dryden praises his friend's combination of virtue and learning, an ideal crystallized by Milton, and one which Dryden would respect throughout his life.

Lines 39-72

Having symbolized the young Hastings as a brilliant star, Dryden requests, rhetorically, that such famous astronomers as Ptolemy and Tycho Brahe attempt to determine the essence of Hastings, although the job, hyperbolically speaking, is of course above their skill. Hastings is viewed again as a bright jewel-studded case on the outside, and a virtuous soul on the inside. (See Commentary.)

Lines 73-108

Dryden returns to his grief for Henry, and suggests that he would have been more famous than any Roman or Greek. Dryden also realizes that his youthful poem may be unequal to the situation he is writing about, but he is compensated by the fact that Henry will be mourned extensively: "The tongue may fail, but overflowing eyes,/ Will weep out lasting streams of elegies" (lines 91-2). Dryden then addresses the "virgin-widow," who represents Hastings' fiancee. (Her father, the "skillful sire" [line 95] had been the attending physician when Hastings died.) Dryden urges Hastings' fiancee to marry Hastings' soul to her own in a platonic union, which will in turn perpetuate the virtue that was crystallized in Hastings.

Comment And Analysis: There is little doubt that Dryden's expression of grief is sincere. We sense that Dryden felt the loss of his friend in a personal fashion and honestly desired to eulogize him in this poem. Dryden unquestionably knew Hastings' fiancee and would therefore have tried to write a poem of which she would be proud. The poem, as Dryden's earliest published work, displays great learning - as is suggested, for example, by the allusion to the astronomers being discussed in contemporary debates, and by the classical allusions to such figures as Seneca, Cato, and Caesar. We do not need to understand all of the various allusions - which range from Archimedes to Ganymede. They are important to us in that they suggest the wide range of reading already behind Dryden as a young man. The poem is an extended development of the metaphor of Lord Hastings as a bright star, a more or less conventional embodiment for a deceased friend. The movement from statement of grief, to praise, and back to grief is a conventional pattern of elegiac poetry.

Form And Style: The form of Dryden's early poem is that of the elegy, and Dryden had undoubtedly read many classical elegiac poems. The style, however, is modeled after that of the "metaphysical" poetry of Donne and Cowley, the latter in particular being one of the young Dryden's most admired poets. There is a great deal of complex, ornate "metaphysical" imagery, for example, when Dryden refers to the smallpox which killed Hastings; the smallpox makes blisters which appear like stars on the box housing his soul:

> Was there no milder way but the smallpox,
> The very filth'ness of Pandora's box?
> So many spots, like noeves, our Venus soil?
> One jewel set off with so many a foil
>
> Blisters with pride swell'd, which thro's flesh did sprout.
> Like rose-buds, stuck i' th'lily skin about.
> Each little pimple had a tear in it,
> To wail the fault its rising did commit
>
> ....
> Or were these gems sent to adorn his skin,
> The cab'net of a richer soul within? (lines 53-64).

The image of a set of smallpox blisters crying out their fluid in protest, and then turning into a group of jewels is a hard image to accept and must be viewed as exemplative of Dryden's poetic immaturity. But we at least see the beginnings of a poetic craftsmanship which would develop later; there is the strong use of the rhetorical device of hyperbole, for example, when Dryden explains how the divine gifts which are generally dispersed through many personalities were all concentrated in Hastings (line 32, ff.). And some couplets are quite powerfully presented, as when Dryden refers to Hastings' death by writing: "But hasty winter, with one blast, hath brought/ The hopes of autumn, summer, spring, to naught" (lines 77-8). The poem also shows us Dryden's early ease at controlling rhyming couplets in iambic pentameter (heroic couplets).

BRIGHT NOTES STUDY GUIDE

"HEROIC STANZAS ON CROMWELL"

Introduction

Dryden wrote his "Heroic Stanzas: Consecrated To The Glorious Memory Of His Most Serene And Renow'd Highness Oliver, Late Lord Protector Of This Commonwealth and Co." toward the end of 1658. Oliver Cromwell died on September 3, 1658 and was buried on November 23. Dryden's poem was written shortly after the funeral. This commendatory poem was printed twice in the following year, once together with Waller and Sprat's poems on the same occasion, simply entitled *Three Poems Upon The Death Of His Late Highness Oliver, Lord Protector of England, Scotland, and Ireland.* It is interesting to note that in 1682, some of Dryden's enemies reprinted the volume with a title page reading *Three Poems Upon The Death of the Late Usurper Oliver Cromwell.* In any case, Dryden's thirty-seven-stanza poem is generally acknowledged to be the first important piece that he wrote.

SUMMARY

Stanzas 1-10

Dryden commences by explaining that it is impossible to describe in words the glory that belongs to Cromwell. This is the conventional method of opening a commendatory poem. Dryden asks, "How shall I then begin, or where conclude,/To draw a fame so truly circular?" (**stanza** 5). No order exists in verse like the order which radiated from Cromwell. Dryden then presents the major **theme** of the poem: Cromwell received his greatness and special abilities from God in Heaven. This central idea is asserted for the first time in the sixth **stanza**, as Dryden writes: "His grandeur he deriv'd from heav'n alone;/For he was great ere fortune made him so." Dryden explains that war only made Cromwell suddenly seem greater; the truth is that he had always been great. Dryden repeats the idea of Cromwell's divine sponsorship in the tenth **stanza** where he writes: "And yet dominion was not his design;/We owe that blessing not to him, but Heaven."

Stanzas 11-26

Dryden explains that whereas former English sovereigns pursued war and enjoyed quarreling, Cromwell loved peace and "fought to end our fighting" (**stanza** 12). For Cromwell, "Peace was the prize of all his toils and care" (**stanza** 16). Ireland and Scotland owe their safety to Cromwell, who blended together love and majesty as an ideal ruler. Dryden continues by mentioning Cromwell's involvement with Holland, France, and Spain, and then explains that everyone was eager to fight by Cromwell's side because virtuous souls leaned to him just as the divining rod points to gold underground.

Stanzas 27-37

Dryden reminds us again that Cromwell derived his "heroic virtue" from heaven (**stanza** 27), and then suggests England's massive indebtedness to Cromwell. In hyperbolic praise, Dryden suggests that Cromwell's deeds were only an inadequate glimpse of the greatness of his soul; Cromwell "own'd a soul above/The highest acts it could produce to show" (**stanza** 32). Dryden is arguing that Cromwell's true greatness went unrevealed, but his deeds and person nevertheless should serve as an example of how heaven blesses the conjunction of "piety and valor" (**stanza** 37).

Comment And Analysis: Perhaps the most important feature of Dryden's stanzas on Cromwell is that they make no specific reference to Cromwell's kind of government. There is no statement about tolerance or democracy, except for the brief mention of being free in stanza 29. Dryden is making the point that Cromwell was sent from Heaven to save England from chaotic disunity. And, Dryden asserts, Cromwell succeeded and thus is a lasting example of virtue wedded to courage. Cromwell, in other words, has become symbolic of ideal man, rather than of any one kind of philosophically considered government.

Form And Style: Dryden uses the stanzaic form of alternating lines rhyming a, b, a, b, in iambic pentameter; that is, he does not use the couplets of his first published poem on Lord Hastings. Dryden's first major poem now shows the influence, not only of Cowley and the metaphysicals, but of Davenant as well. The style of the "Heroic Stanzas" is relatively simple, and certainly much simpler than his earlier poem. Again we find Dryden relying on the use of hyperbole, noticeably in stanzas 6 and 32. Both suggest that although some of Cromwell's greatness could be seen, it was nevertheless only a suggestion of his larger unseen greatness. Dryden has chosen to celebrate Cromwell in a style designed to match the simplicity of Cromwell himself. There is little "metaphysical" imagery and the poem is easily understood. Furthermore, in contrast to the lines on Hastings written earlier, there is much less reliance on classical and scholarly allusion.

THE POETRY OF JOHN DRYDEN

"ASTRAEA REDUX"

Introduction

Less than two years after writing his heroic **stanzas** in praise of Cromwell, Dryden again took up his pen, this time to celebrate the return of Charles II to the English throne. The result was Astraea Redux, "A Poem On The Happy Restoration And Return Of His Sacred Majesty Charles The Second." Charles arrived in England on May 25, 1660 and Dryden's poem was written at about that time. *Astraea Redux* (meaning "justice returned") was first published by Herringman, who was to remain Dryden's publisher and friend, for nineteen years. Herringman reprinted Dryden's *Astraea Redux* with *To His Sacred Majesty* and *Annus Mirabilis* in 1688.

SUMMARY

Lines 1-60

Dryden opens the poem by explaining how, while the rest of the world enjoyed a general peace, England was experiencing a dreadful quiet. Dryden discusses the state of affairs under Cromwell's provisional government and suggests that it was not a satisfactory situation for England. Church and state had been thrown into confusion; factions had surrounded both pulpit and throne, but "the rebel," Cromwell, was able to endure. Dryden, who only recently had eulogized Cromwell, now refers to his "rabble" following; England, Dryden feels, needs to be ruled once again with more discipline; because Charles II was great enough to "live above his banishment," England will be in secure hands when he resumes leadership.

Lines 61-124

Dryden discusses the unfortunate way in which Charles II had previously been "Forc'd into exile from his rightful throne," and then argues that Charles will be, like Christ (indirectly implied), better able to reign because he passed heroically through suffering; his experience is perhaps typical of how "We light in dark afflictions find." Dryden mentions Charles II's "famous grandsire," Henry IV of France (Charles' maternal grandfather). Dryden asserts that with the new leadership, England will once again be strong and "Our lion now will foreign foes avail."

Lines 125-213

Dryden explains that in Charles' absence, England has been in a frost, and now, with his return, is thawing. Dryden refers to the way in which Sir George Booth (line 145) had, after Cromwell's death, urged that Charles assume leadership, but he was defeated because Heaven had not yet decided for Charles to come: "Heav'n's prefixed hour (had) not come." Dryden speaks of General George Monk (line 151), a leader of the English forces in Scotland, who played a significant part in the restoration of Charles to the English throne. His help was guided by "Providence" and observed by the "Saints." Dryden refers to Monk's military expertise as "not the hasty product of a day,/But the well-ripen'd fruit of wise delay." Previously, England had behaved like a silly young girl in love, but now she's beginning to behave like a mature woman; having passed, like Charles, through suffering, England is better equipped to appreciate its new "bliss."

Lines 214-255

Dryden acknowledges Charles' heavenly as well as his earthly parentage. He urges Charles therefore to "find/Revenge less sweet than a forgiving mind," that is, to overlook England's previous rejection. Dryden, in flattery, asserts that Charles' goodness is the only thing greater than the laws. England's tears fall in expiation for its guilt. Dryden refers to Charles' arrival to England in May and then to the mysterious star which appeared on Charles' birthday, May 29, 1630 - a star which had been the subject of much contemporary debate among English astrologers. In any case, the poem concludes by declaring that now that England is once again happily united, she can exert her influence over the world and her empire can grow. England will enjoy a growth in both arms and art. England will again be, in short, a great nation.

Comment And Analysis: Astraea Redux has, deservedly, enjoyed a less favorable reputation than Dryden's "Heroic Stanzas." The reasons are not difficult to discern. Astraea Redux is a more or less ordinary poem; there is nothing startling or surprising in it. Dryden simply retells the story of Charles' exile and return. In mythology, the goddess of Justice, named Astraea, departed from earth to heaven when the Iron Age arrived. Dryden's idea is that with the return of Charles, a Golden Age will be established and Astraea will return to earth: through Charles, justice will be restored. The idea behind the poem is thus relatively simple.

As in the "Heroic Stanzas," Dryden has again chosen to focus on the man rather than on the man's political

position. Charles, like Cromwell in the earlier poem, is depicted as a leader sent to England by Divine Providence. There is no expressed endorsement of any one particular political opinion, except in as much as Dryden thinks the country is ready for a firmer kind of government. Dryden's reference to the public as the "vulgar" and the "rabble," reveals a more aristocratic, or simply less democratic attitude than that discovered in the stanzas on Cromwell.

Form And Style: Dryden's Astraea Redux is, of course, written in heroic couplets (of rhyming iambic pentameter). It is not longer than some of his late poems, but it certainly is the longest poem he had yet written. This length in itself may explain the poem's rather disjointed, rambling, gossipy manner. The style is more elaborate than that used to write about Cromwell, as Dryden once again presents various difficult (and sometimes irrelevant) images. There seems to be a large amount of superfluous discussion and the allusions are not sudden and to the point. The poem as a whole has a somewhat loose style which makes it less enjoyable to read than Dryden's other early poems.

ESSAY QUESTIONS AND ANSWERS

Question: Was it unscrupulous of Dryden to praise Charles in *Astraea Redux* after having so eagerly praised Cromwell in "Heroic Stanzas?"

Answer: No. Dryden believed deeply that poetry was more important than politics. There is no denying, of course, that

Dryden was an opportunist who changed with the times. He celebrated Cromwell when the country did, and he welcomed Charles when the country did. In other words, all of England had to undergo a change of heart with its change in leadership. Granted, not everyone in England wrote a poem celebrating Charles' return. But Dryden was an aspiring poet. He viewed Charles' return as an event of substantial national interest and therefore worthy of being treated in a poem. Dryden was concerned with a poetic event, not with the actual triumph of any one political philosophy.

Question: What is the essential stylistic orientation of the young Dryden's poetry?

Answer: Dryden's early inclination lay toward delicately balanced rhythms. He writes in a very tight metrical pattern of iambic pentameter verse. His use of heroic **couplets** in "Upon The Death of Henry, Lord Hastings," and in *Astraea Redux* shows that even in his early career as a poet, Dryden had a natural ability to write rhyming poetry. Although we of course are aware of the breadth of Dryden's early broad learning, we are most aware of his facility for meter and **rhyme**. This talent also eclipses his less admirable attempts to imitate the conceits (complex images) of the "**metaphysical**" poets, Donne and Cowley. For while Dryden is experimenting with different kinds of images, he seems steadfast in-his pursuit of excellence in **rhyme**. There is less metrical experimentation than perfection of existing forms. This early control of rhymed **couplets** should be considered the most outstanding feature of the apprentice poetry of Dryden.

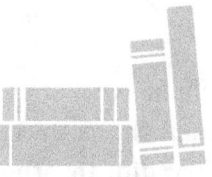

ANNUS MIRABILIS

Introduction

Dryden's three-hundred-stanza poem *Annus Mirabilis* was published in 1667 with the full title of "Annus Mirabilis, The Year of Wonder, 1666, An Historical Poem Containing The Progress and Various Successes of Our Naval War With Holland, Under the Conduct of His Highness Prince Rupert, And His Grace The Duke of Albemarle, And Describing The Fire of London." Although to the modern reader this title appears to be a joke, Dryden undoubtedly thought it a good summary of the poem.

Dryden dedicates the poem to London, the metropolis of Great Britain. Dryden claims a parallel between his poem's being the first poem dedicated to a city and London's being the first city of the world. London has not only endured, but actually triumphed over, a series of horrible afflictions, and therefore she deserves to be celebrated in verse. In the dedication, as later in the poem, London is presented as a phoenix rising out of its ashes - a convenient **metaphor** for a city which has just been in flames for four days. Dryden's dedication is, conventionally, little more than a gratuitous and necessary explanation of why the poem was written. But in a letter to The Honorable Sir Robert Howard, Dryden explains in detail what he has tried to do in *Annus Mirabilis*.

In this long letter, Dryden explains the way in which he has described the war in the first half of the poem and the great London fire in the second. He explains his selection of a **rhyme** scheme: "I have chosen to write my poem in quatrains, or **stanzas** of four in alternate **rhyme**, because I have ever judg'd them more noble, and of greater dignity, both for the sound and number, than any other verse in use amongst us...I have always found the **couplet** verse most easy (tho' not so proper for this occasion) for there the work is sooner at an end, every two lines concluding the labor of the poet." Dryden, in other words, feels that it is easier to write couplets, but that for certain occasions, the use of "quatrains" is more appropriate. Dryden explains his feelings about his endeavors in the actual writing of the poem. He writes, "I have never yet seen the description of any naval fight in the proper terms which are us'd at sea...for my own part, if I had little knowledge of the sea, yet I have thought it no shame to learn." Dryden, in short, confesses that his knowledge and vocabulary of the sea had to be enlarged before he could write *Annus Mirabilis*.

Theory Of Wit

But more important than the specific remarks Dryden makes about the poem in his long preface is his famous statement of literary theory regarding wit:

> **The composition of all poems is, or ought to be, of wit; and wit in the poet...is no other than the faculty of imagination in the writer, which, like a nimble spaniel, beats over and ranges thro' the field of memory, till it springed the quarry it hunted after... wit written is that which is well defin'd, the happy result of thought, or product of imagination. But to**

proceed from wit, in the general notion of it, to the proper wit of an heroic or historical poem, I judge it chiefly to consist in the delightful imaging of persons, actions, passions, or things.

Dryden, in short, makes conscious intellectual development one of the requirements of poetry. And the kind of "wit" that he discusses is amply illustrated in the bulk of his poems. Dryden continues this famous discussion of wit by saying that it "is some lively and apt description, dress'd in such colors of speech that it sets before your eyes the absent object as perfectly and more delightfully than nature."

Annus Mirabilis is a poem designed to inspire a nation. Dryden is arguing that the 1666 war and the fire were not acts of God punishing the English people, but rather trials for them to endure. At this time in England there was great confusion, doubt, and fear that the country was drifting toward further rebellion. There had appeared a series of seditious pamphlets, and Dryden, in his long poem dedicated to London, is deliberately trying to counteract them.

SUMMARY

Stanzas 1-15

Dryden begins the poem by referring to the way in which Holland has grown in arts at home, while becoming cruel in matters of trade abroad. Holland has selfishly limited the trade enjoyed by other nations like England. Dryden then makes an analogy between the relationship which exists between Holland and England and the relationship existing between Carthage and Rome: In the Punic War, Rome had defeated Carthage, because although Carthage was wealthier, Rome was stronger; in the same fashion, England will overpower the wealthy Holland. The peace between the two countries has only been artificial, and the king, as the leader of a nation crying out for war, has decided to wage war against the Dutch.

Stanzas 16-30

Dryden immediately plunges the reader into the midst of the massive naval war between England and Holland. We hear of the heroic struggling of the Duke of York, and then of York's Vice-Admiral, Sir John Lawson (who had been well known as a fighter, both in the Commonwealth and in the Restoration). In **stanza** 21, Dryden compares Lawson to Protesilaus who, as the first Greek to rush upon the Trojan shore, was the first one killed: "He first was kill'd who first to battle went." Dryden then mentions the way in which the Admiral of Holland, "their chief," was blown up; the Dutch, sensing the presence of heaven, withdrew to ports where their badly battered ships could be repaired. At this point some Dutch ships from India appear, filled with "all the riches of the rising sun" (i.e., the East), but these ships are pursued and attacked by the English ships. Dryden's poetry becomes active:

These fight like husbands, but like lovers those:
  These fain would keep, and those more fain enjoy;

And to such height their frantic passion grows,
  That what both love, both hazard to destroy.

Stanzas 31-45

Dryden pauses to make a series of **didactic** remarks about wealth, and about domestic relations. He forms a philosophy which he will echo later in the poem: metaphorically, there are shipwrecks everywhere in life: "Such are the proud designs of humankind,/And so we suffer shipwreck everywhere."

Dryden explains that until this point in the war, the two nations of England and Holland had been the only participating nations. Now, however, "That eunuch guardian of rich Holland's trade" - France, who envies England - has sided with Holland; once France has entered, Denmark also joins Holland. (Historically, France and Denmark had declared war on England in the early part of 1666.) Dryden explains how Louis XIV of France ("Lewis") had chased the English from his shore, while Charles II "the French subjects did invite." That is, upon the declaration of war, Louis XIV banished all English citizens from France, while in contrast, Charles II offered asylum and religious toleration for any Frenchman who came to England. Dryden explains that Charles II engaged in the war against the three countries fearlessly.

Stanzas 46-60

Dryden mentions the "doubled charge" - the large amounts of money for the war granted to the king by the English Parliament. Then we hear of two new naval chiefs who will dominate the rest of the poem: Prince Rupert, who was the nephew of Charles I and had fought in the civil wars, and

Duke Albemarle, who was George Monk in Dryden's *Astraea Redux*. The two new chiefs sail off to battle, but their fleets are divided.

Historically, Prince Rupert had been ordered to take seventy men-of-war (ships) and engage a group of French ships that were supposedly approaching. He and Duke Albemarle sailed in different directions. The report of the French ships proved to be false; instead, Albemarle encountered a much larger force of Dutch ships, and England suffered a costly blow. But Duke Albemarle, nevertheless, fought valiantly, despite the fact that he had only fifty ships against the Dutch De Ruyter, who commanded seventy-six. Dryden narrates:

> **The duke, less numerous, but in courage more,**
> **On wings of all the winds to combat flies:**
> **His murdering guns a loud defiance roar,**
> **And bloody crosses on his flagstaffs rise.**

Dryden describes their fighting further, comparing them to struggling Olympic champions.

Stanzas 61-75

Dryden continues his description of Albemarle's fight. He explains how "heroes of old" sought shelter when they were wounded, while Albemarle only fights harder and turns his ship directly into the Dutch. The strength of the English fleet is rejuvenated rather than lessened by the increasing intensity of battle: all day the English charge and recharge. Then night arrives:

> The night comes on, we eager to pursue
>   The combat still, and they asham'd to leave:
> Till the last streaks of dying day withdrew,
>   And doubtful moonlight did our rage deceive.

At each turn, the English are depicted as having greater strength and courage than the Dutch. In one of the most imaginative **stanzas** of the poem, Dryden suggests that the English even enjoy dreaming of battle at night:

> In the English fleet each ship resounds with joy,
>   And loud applause of their great leader's fame:
> In fiery dreams the Dutch they still destroy,
>   And, slumb'ring, smile at the imagin'd flame.

The Dutch, in contrast, lie stretched out on the decks of their ships like weary oxen.

Stanzas 76-90

The Dutch, again in contrast to the English, have nightmares, in which they wander over fearful precipices or walk among the dead in dark churches. Dryden then takes us into the second day of battle. The Dutch, though exhausted, are happy to hear some reinforcements are coming (historically, sixteen additional men-of-war). Albemarle, realizing that a bigger battle looms on the horizon, orders his wounded men ashore and tells the rest that the "fortune of Great Britain" rests in their forthcoming performance. His words of council to his men summarize the spirit of the entire war: "courage from hearts, and not from numbers, grows." The English Navy wanders through the hordes of Belgian ships like a bird lost in the woods. Dryden imaginatively pictures the English among the Dutch as "the swordfish in the whale," stabbing wherever possible. The Dutch attack from all sides, noticeably from the rear, and at each turn the "little fleet grows less." Albemarle, unhappy at the loss of so many men, vows to fight until he can bring his ships to safety.

Stanzas 91-105

Albemarle draws his ships tightly together to move as a single unit, which, by firing its many canons creates a protective smoke screen. In this fashion, Albemarle is able to lead his ships safely through the Dutch ships, just as the Israelites, surrounded by clouds, had stolen out of Egypt. An enemy ship approaches, but when it is quickly sunk, the others are too afraid to come near. Albemarle reflects on the last two times that the Dutch had been beaten by the English, and then he contemplates his own probable death:

Yet like an English gen'ral will I die,
  And all the ocean make my spacious grave:
Women and cowards on the land may lie;
  The sea's a tomb that's proper for the brave.

Then, as the third day of battle opens, Albemarle sees Prince Rupert and his ships coming to aid them.

Stanzas 106-120

Prince Rupert has heard the cannons and guessed that the English were overmatched by the Dutch; therefore he has hastened to the aid of his good friend Albemarle, in the same way that an eagle comes to the rescue of its young. The Dutch are depicted as "fall'n angels" trying to entice and trap the new foe, but they are unable to, and instead fear "This new Messiah's coming." Dryden has deliberately suggested that the war between the English and the Dutch was like the war between Heaven and Hell, or between Satan and Christ. In any case, Rupert's actions are all guided by "Heroic virtue." Finally he is happily united with Albemarle, and on the morning of the fourth day, they sail together into battle.

Stanzas 121-135

The Dutch and the English continue to wage war; Rupert singles out a pair of favorite Dutch ships, which he begins to attack; but at the last moment one of the Dutch ships fires a shot which topples Rupert's center mast. Then all three ships lie idly by each other, until the Dutch ships sail away.

Stanzas 136-150

As the Dutch steal away, Rupert watches wistfully. Dryden then turns to a description of the various ways in which the battle-wearied ships are now repaired. New foundations are laid, bullets are picked out of the wood, and new pitch is poured into sagging seams. The **stanzas** reflect Dryden's study of the arts of ship-building and ship repair before writing the poem.

Stanzas 151-165

Dryden describes the Loyal London, a new vessel, built to replace a destroyed one which had simply been called the London; the new ship has been given to "their best-lov'd king," Charles II, by the city. The construction of this new ship suggests to Dryden the interesting components of the whole art of ship-building; he thus offers a digression concerning shipping and navigation, beginning:

By viewing Nature, Nature's handmaid Art
   Makes mighty things from small beginning grow:
Thus fishes first to shipping did impart
   Their tall the rudder, and their head the prow.

This section includes a passage that is particularly interesting to the modern reader, where Dryden discusses the new creation of a unified world and imagines a day when man will be joined in the air, just as ships have now joined men on earth.

Stanzas 166-180

Dryden makes a short apostrophe to the Royal Society, an organization founded for the advancement of scientific learning in 1660. But what is most important is that the English "endure" the toils of war and redeem the seas "from th'injurious Dutch." For the Dutch ships have now come closer to England's shores, and the size of the Dutch fleet has daily grown larger. (Historically, the Dutch Navy needed to make fewer repairs after this battle, and thus they were back on the sea before the English were. But the English did not delay long.) Dryden names some of the English leaders now returning to sea - Allen, Holems, Sprag, etc. But, besides the well-known names, there are thousands of men that some other nobler poem will adorn; as far as Dryden knows, everyone who was British and fighting for Rupert fought well. In any case, the enlarged and restored English fleet goes to sea. The Dutch, seeing its size, decide to retreat from the shore, and instead, set a trap for the British:

The wary Dutch this gathering storm foresaw,
  And durst not bide it on the English coast:
Behind their treach'rous shallos they withdraw,
  And there lay snares to catch the British host.
So the false spider, when her nets are spread,
  Deep ambushed in her silent den does lie,
And feels far off the trembling of her thread,
  Whose filmy chord should bind the struggling fly.

Stanzas 181-195

Dryden elaborates on the Dutch hopes of ensnaring the English ships. But the English suddenly catch up with the Dutch and square off next to them. For the first time, the Dutch seem to be fighting for the sake of honor. Yet, in spite of their new courage, the Dutch are unable to repel the English, who fight as if there were an Albemarle or a Rupert aboard every ship. Dryden refers to the "famous leader of the Belgian fleet," De Ruyter.

Stanzas 196-210

Dryden summarizes the conclusion of the battle and explains the final actions of the victorious English ships - for example, the burning of the Dutch fleet in the *Vlie* by Sir Robert Holmes. The English did a certain amount of dishonorable pillaging: "greedy seamen rummage every hold" and like bad priests, take what they want for themselves and sacrifice the rest. Dryden is expressing his disapproval of this final chapter of the story of the war. Then he goes on to present a transition from the first subject of the poem - the English-Dutch Naval War - to the second subject, the great London fire of 1666:

> Swell'd with our late successes on the foe,
> > Which France and Holland wanted power to cross,
> We urge an unseen fate to lay us low,
> > And feed their envious eyes with English loss.

Dryden seems to believe that the fire is a kind of punishment for the irreputable behavior of the English following their victory over the Dutch.

Stanzas 211-225

Dryden carefully reconstructs, in highly poetic language, the events of the great fire of London. The fire began mysteriously in the night and slowly grew to large proportions and ravaged the city. Dryden writes:

> In this deep quiet, from what source unknown,
> > Those seeds of fire their fatal birth disclose;
> And first, few scatt'rings sparks about were blown,
> > Big with the flames that to our ruins rose.

The "infant monster" grew into a pillaging beast, and was released on the city like a gigantic prisoner bursting from imprisonment. Dryden graphically mentions ghosts coming from the London bridge where the heads of traitors were usually placed on stakes.

Stanzas 226-240

Dryden enlarges his description of the fire as it rages larger and travels along the river banks. The fire becomes personified:

> The fire, meantime, walks in broader gross;
>   To either hand his wings he opens wide:
> He wades the streets, and straight he reaches cross,
>   And plays his longing flames on th'other side.

Dryden also describes the fire as if it were a challenging military opponent, thus drawing a close parallel between the war and the fire as both beleaguers of London. Dryden then goes on to introduce a picture of the suffering of King Charles II, who is depicted as sleepless, disturbed, and filled with pity.

Stanzas 241-255

When he has finished discussing the king's despair, Dryden comments on the way in which the poor people covetously regard the spoils of the wealthy. In times of tragedy, human nature - particularly the appetite of greed - is sometimes seen more clearly than in times of peace. Dryden writes of the scavengers:

> The rich grow suppliant, and the poor grow proud;
>   Those offer mighty gain, and these ask more:
> So void of pity is the ignoble crowd,
>   When others' ruin may increase their store.

Dryden refers philosophically to the way in which people who live by the shore eagerly await shipwrecks. This reference returns us to the philosophy of life's shipwrecks, presented in the first half of the poem. Now, in a parallel emotion, people run into burning houses to steal whatever they can find, while in the meantime, miserable homeowners hopelessly observe the approach of destruction.

Stanzas 256-270

Dryden describes further the suffering of the people as they watch their possessions being destroyed by the fire. Some people are nervously stirring up the coals, while others lie in the dewy fields with their children. The only hope that the people have is their knowledge that King Charles cares about them and is suffering with them:

No thought can ease them but their sovereign's care,
    Whose praise th'afflicted as their comfort sing:
Ev'n those whom want might drive to just despair,
    Think life a blessing under such a king.

And Dryden continues by actually describing the king in his grief:

Meantime he sadly suffers in their grief,
    Out-weeps an hermit, and out-prays a saint:
All the long night he studies their relief,
    How they may be supplied, and how may want.

Dryden presents the "king's prayer," as we listen to Charles imploring God to have mercy on England and change the course of this devastating fire. Charles refers to his conscientious care of the country as a reason for God to stop the fire.

Stanzas 271-285

Dryden explains that the king's prayer was heard in heaven. In response, the "eternal choir" select a cherub to drive the fire away from the English ammunition store. The fire has now been raging for four days and nights. Finally, God looks down on London with pity and decides to extinguish the fire:

At length th'Almighty cast a pitying eye,
　And mercy softly touched his melting breast:
He saw the town's one half in rubbish lie,
　And eager flames drive on to storm the rest.

An hollow crystal pyramid he takes,
　In firmamental waters dipp'd above;
Of it a broad extinguisher he makes
　And hoods the flames that to their quarry strove.

When God applies this bizarrely imagined, colossal fire extinguisher, the last flames begin to recede. The king beholds this phenomenon and, bowing down on the ground with heartfelt thanks, acknowledges God's assistance.

Stanzas 286-304

The king opens up his large store of food to feed the people, who have of course remained loyal to him throughout their unhappiness. Out of the ashes of her destruction, London, phoenix-like, rises as a greater city than she had been before. Once like a naive shepherdess, she is now more "like a maiden queen" who will have distinguished suitors from around the world. By comparison, no other city is as great as London. She has undergone affliction courageously and emerged successfully as an experienced, wonderful city; this has, indeed, been her "year of wonders."

Comment And Analysis: *Annus Mirabilis*, **though not one of Dryden's best poems, is important for a variety of reasons. In the first place, we see that Dryden is**

able to write a long, heroic poem, and to sustain a unified discussion of hardship and triumph. But more importantly, Dryden has effectively accomplished what he hoped to accomplish: he has rallied popular support around King Charles II. Dryden paints a flattering picture of a very human and conscientious king. Charles suffers greatly when the fire breaks out and finally prays to God for assistance because God has aided him in his past exile and hardships. Charles, in short, is seen as a compassionate, understanding king who loves his people and his country. The poem was designed by Dryden to bolster England's national morale and to rebuff the Republican critics of Charles - and this is exactly what the poem successfully accomplished.

Annus Mirabilis is a poem of heroic suffering followed by heroic triumph. London is redeemed, is taken out of the jaws of disaster and crowned as the first city of the world. The two events of war and fire are hardships which England must endure as part of her passage to greatness. The year 1666 is seen as a year of "trial," not as a year of punishment for England. If God were merely displaying his anger, he would probably not have allowed England to win the war (and thus to defeat Holland for the third time). God is on King Charles' side and therefore Charles was successful in carrying the war to victory and in extinguishing the fire. Charles, we must remember, is not only a king by divine right; he has the sanction of his people as well, for they recalled him from exile to rule England. As a great king, it is fitting that Charles be confronted by great adversaries; he is that much more victorious. The year 1666 is his own as well as London's "year of wonder."

We must not underestimate the importance of *Annus Mirabilis* as a Christian allegory. The English are on the side of God and the Dutch are on the side of the devil. The naval war is one between good and evil. There are various references to the way in which the Dutch fear Heaven's intervention against them; Rupert, we recall, arrives like a second Messiah; at the same point in the poem, the Dutch are referred to as fallen angels. The two tests of war and fire can be seen as tests of Christian courage and fortitude. England, like Christ, must suffer before she can successfully reign. That God finally extinguishes the fire is Dryden's way of saying that God has decided that England has had enough. God will therefore be merciful, as Charles has been a merciful king.

Form And Style: Dryden explained that he wrote in quatrains of alternating rhyme because he thought them best suited to his subject. Dryden probably realized that a long poem (300 stanzas) should not be written in couplets because it would seem tedious. Interestingly enough, however, Dryden must have found the writing of *Annus Mirabilis* difficult, because he never used the quatrain form again.

Dryden thought of *Annus Mirabilis* as an historical poem rather than an epic primarily because his poem did not (and could not) have unity of action. The structure of the poem is simply one of two connected halves: a description of the English-Dutch War and a description of the London fire. However, it is important to realize that Dryden has not written two poems and grouped them under one title, for he has carefully related the two halves of his poem to one another. Thematically, they are of course connected as a twin pair of evil threats - and even as "temptations" - which were both posed for England within one year. But more important, they are connected by way of poetic style. There is an intermingling of the language of the sea with the language of fire: for example, when Dryden pauses in the middle of the fire to offer a philosophical comment on shipwrecks - to remind us, in other words, of his earlier reference to shipwrecks. The fire of London is, like the war, one large metaphorical shipwreck.

Dryden's language of the sea shows a learned familiarity with navigation; he easily uses words like "sheets," "sails," "turrets," "tack," "rigging," "hulls," etc. His full knowledge of ships is perhaps best seen in his digression on the arts of ship-building and ship repair (stanza 155, ff.) Mixed with the conventional words of the sea, however, are certain creative expressions which originate in Dryden: he refers to ships in stanza 57, for example, as "sea-built forts."

Dryden weaves a distinct classicism into *Annus Mirabilis*. There are continuous references to such characters as Patroclus, Xenophon, and Caesar, as well as the larger, sustained parallel between the English-Dutch War and the Roman-Carthaginian (Punic) war. Many of Dryden's heroic statements, particularly those describing the valor of Rupert and Albemarle, are heightened in gravity by way of classical allusion; there are frequent echoes of Virgil's Aeneid.

> Again we should realize that Dryden relates the second half of the poem to the first largely by way of poetic language. He describes the fire with the same kinds of words that he used to describe the sea; the fire, like the battleships, "pursues," or "retreats." As for the fire's smoke: "the curling billows roll their restless tide." The winds blow the fire no less heartily than they had previously blown the ships. In other words, through his maintenance of the language of the sea, Dryden makes the two parts of the poem fit tightly together.

ESSAY QUESTIONS AND ANSWERS

Question: What is the symbolism of the vessel named the Loyal London?

Answer: *Annus Mirabilis* is a poem devoted to the death and rebirth of a city. In other words, London is momentarily battered. It is plagued by fire and war in one year and, in effect, crumbles under the affliction. But out of its ashes, London rises up again to become an even more powerful metropolis than she was before. The new London, furthermore, is loyal. Where before there had been civil wars and internal chaos, now London has rallied loyally around King Charles II because he dutifully stayed with the country through its perils and torment. Dryden wrote the poem to end Republican criticism; it is thus appropriate that Dryden point out the "loyal" nature of the new London built to replace the old. The ship, Dryden tells us, is given to Charles by the people and thus symbolizes the unity of national sentiment.

Question: What is the meaning of Dryden's apostrophe to the Royal Society?

Answer: Dryden was very interested in the work of the Royal Society and in science in general. With his broad intellectual interests, he had joined the Royal Society early in its life (it was founded in 1660), and had maintained an interest in scientific advancement. In *Annus Mirabilis*, he directly acknowledges the Royal Society (lines 657-664) as a benefit to humanity. Throughout the poem, there are also various scientific references: There is his **allusion** to the circulation of blood (**stanza** 2); to the unctuous exhalations of the sun (**stanza** 17); to the mining of minerals (stanza 139). (But despite Dryden's apostrophe to the Royal Society, he did not maintain his membership past late 1666, when he was dropped for not paying his dues.)

THE SATIRES

ABSALOM AND ACHITOPHEL

Introduction

With *Absalom and Achitophel*, Dryden launches the first of three great political **satires** - the other two are *The Medal* and *Mac Flecknoe* - all of which have contributed to Dryden's popularity. All three poems contain incisive, scathing, satirical portraits of Dryden's enemies. After the "popish plot" (see Introduction) had quieted down, there were successive attempts to put through Parliament the so-called "Exclusion Bill," which would exclude Catholics from the English throne. Such a bill would automatically prevent Charles II's brother, James - the Duke of York and the legitimate heir - from becoming king after Charles. At the same time, a group of Protestant nobles, headed by the famous Whig, the Earl of Shaftesbury, was attempting to make Charles II's illegitimate but Protestant son, the Duke of Monmouth, the next king. Although King Charles liked his son, he did not like the concept of interrupting the legal line of succession. Public sentiment supported his position, and Charles brought the Earl of Shaftesbury before him with the serious charge of high treason. Dryden wrote *Absalom and Achitophel* at the request of the king, who wanted it published the week before Shaftesbury's arraignment. (In spite of Dryden's work, Shaftesbury was released.)

Dryden decided to transcribe a scriptural story from the Old Testament into the contemporary political scene. The idea of using the story of *Absalom and Achitophel* was probably suggested to him by an anonymously written tract entitled Absalom's *Conspiracy, or The Tragedy of Treason*, which had appeared in 1680, the same year that Dryden began his poem. (He probably completed it in 1681, releasing it during the week prior to Shaftesbury's trial.) Although published anonymously, most people knew that it was written by Dryden.

Biblical Parallels

The story of *Absalom and Achitophel* is found in II Samuel, 13-16. In brief, the story runs as follows: David, the king of Israel, is challenged by a rebellion spearheaded by Absalom, one of his illegitimate sons. Absalom is advised in his rebellion by a scheming friend named Achitophel, who has always hated the government of David. The king is successful in thwarting his son's rebellion. Then, against the king's wishes, the son is killed.

The way in which Dryden employs the Biblical story as a parallel to the political intrigue of his day is relatively simple, and in any case, logical. Israel and Jerusalem represent England and London - the Jews are, of course, the English - Hebron is Scotland and Egypt is France; Gath is Brussels, where Charles II had been in exile before he was recalled to be king. The Sanhedrin is the English Parliament and the Solymaean rout the London rabble. The Anglican clergy are represented by the Jewish rabbins, the Presbyterians by the Levites. Throughout, of course, the English are "the chosen people," while the Catholics are heathen.

With respect to characters, the parallels are easily remembered: King David of Israel quite aptly represents King Charles II of England; David's illegitimate son, Absalom, represents Charles II's illegitimate son, the Duke of Monmouth; Achitophel is the scheming Earl of Shaftesbury. One of the most wonderfully drawn characters is Zimri, representing Villiers, the Duke of Buckingham, who had satirized Dryden in his play, The Rehearsal. Among the other minor characters are Bathsheba, who symbolizes Charles' mistress, the Duchess of Portsmouth; Saul, who represents Cromwell; and Barzillai, who is Charles' friend and advisor, the Duke of Ormond.

Some Anomalous Parallels

In the second section of the poem - Dryden's account of Achitophel's temptation of Absalom - we have a further religious allegory: King David (Charles II) is viewed as God, his son Absalom (Monmouth) as Christ, and Achitophel (Shaftesbury) as Satan. There are a variety of anomalies in this set of parallels, perhaps chief of which is the suggestion that Absalom, in his pomp and rebellion, is anything like Christ. In any case, what must be remembered is that *Absalom and Achitophel*, with its explicit political base, contemporary relevance, and allegorical struggle between good and evil is a wonderful poem in its own right; that is, it can be enjoyed without a complete knowledge of who represents whom. The poem is filled with imagination in its treatment of delicate and sometimes comic relationships. Furthermore, the poem has an undeniably brilliant unity which is as much the result of craftsmanship as it is a reflection of the events discussed.

THE POETRY OF JOHN DRYDEN

Dryden enjoyed writing **satire**, and there is a certain amount of relish in his preface to *Absalom and Achitophel*. He writes, for example, "'Tis not my intention to make an apology for my poem...yet if a poem have a genius, it will force its own reception in the world; for there's a sweetness in good verse, which tickles even while it hurts, and no man can be heartily angry with him who pleases him against his will." Dryden was quite explicit when he explained his feelings about **satire**: "I can write severely," he wrote, "with more ease than I can gently. I have but laugh'd at some men's follies, when I could have declaim'd against their vices...the true end of **satire** is the amendment of vices by correction." This sentiment was more or less endorsed by Alexander Pope, who later wrote that **satire** healed with morals what it hurt with wit.

SUMMARY

Lines 1-84

Dryden opens the poem by referring to the custom of polygamy, thinking back humorously to the days "when man on many multiplied his kind." This earthy discussion is designed to introduce the circumstances of the birth of one of King David's illegitimate sons, Absalom (the Duke of Monmouth). Of all the king's children - begotten variously by both wives and slaves - Absalom was the most beautiful and the bravest, perhaps because, Dryden jests, "inspired by some diviner lust,/His father got him with a greater gust." King David loved his son Absalom so much that he was blind to his faults. David rules over Sion (London) peacefully. Dryden makes some humorous remarks about the Jews (the English):

> The Jews, a headstrong, moody murm'ring race,
> As ever tried th'extent and stretch of grace;
> God's pamper'd people, whom, debauch'd with ease,
> No king could govern, nor no God could please.

Dryden continues by explaining how the English first wanted, and then did not want, liberty. As soon as Saul (Cromwell) was dead, the English rejected the idea of making Ishbosheth (Richard Cromwell) the king, while they recalled the exiled Charles II from Huron. The English were tired of civil wars and general dissension and thus wanted to maintain the status quo; however, when there is no specific reason for trouble, "the careful Devil is still at hand with means" to create trouble for both commonwealths and kings.

Lines 85-149

Dryden discusses the old inhabitants of Jerusalem (London) - the Jebusites, who represent the Catholics, or Papists. Once powerful, they now have become weak and are discontented and annoyed at their having to submit to King David's government. David (Charles II) raised the taxes on Catholic land and thus the Catholic priests, represented as "the heathen priesthood," are outraged and of course jealous of the "popish plot," "the nation's curse." The "popish plot" was a plan, first revealed by a man named Titus Oates, to murder Charles and make James the king and the agent of the Jesuits. A French army would aid in the suppression of Protestantism. The "popish plot" may merely have been a rumor that had been crudely digested by the multitude. Dryden refers to the Catholic's alliance with France (Egypt), but then points out that the plot "fail'd for want of common sense." Nevertheless, because of the plot, many opposing factions appeared, and many of them included in their ranks men whom Charles himself had elevated to eminent positions: "rais'd in pow'r and public office high."

Lines 150-219

Dryden introduces the leader of this group of antagonists to his kingship as we meet the title character, Achitophel. The latter of course represents Anthony Ashley Cooper (1621-83), the first Earl of Shaftesbury, who many historians feel was a great man. Shaftesbury was active in both military and financial contributions to England's various governments during his lifetime. From 1678 on, however, Shaftesbury exploited the anti-Catholicism created by the "popish plot" and placed his support behind the Exclusion Bill which would prevent James from following Charles to the throne.

Coleridge thought that in Dryden's evolutionary depiction of Achitophel, each line added to, or modified, the overall character. In any case, Dryden's satirical opening clearly expresses his negative feelings about Shaftesbury:

> **Of these the false Achitophel was first;**
> **A name to all succeeding ages curst:**
> **For close designs and crooked counsels fit;**
> **Sagacious, bold, and turbulent of wit;**
> **Restless, unfix'd in principles and place;**
> **In pow'r unpleased, impatient of disgrace.**

As Dryden continues his satirical attack on Shaftesbury, we should notice one of his most famous and often quoted couplets: "Great wits are sure to madness near allied,/And thin partitions do their bounds divide." Dryden discusses the way in which the ambitious, restless Achitophel, "resolv'd to ruin or to rule the State," exploits public opinion and tries to increase the resistance to the king. As Dryden says of Achitophel: "But wild Ambition loves to slide, not stand,/ And Fortune's ice prefers to Virtue's land." Thus Shaftesbury (Achitophel) "stood at bold defiance with his prince" and even goes so far as to prove the King a Jebusite (Catholic), which was not particularly wrong, for Charles II did in fact confess on his deathbed that he was a Catholic. In any case, Achitophel is determined to bring a new king to the throne; as Dryden facetiously notes, the English tend to change their king every twenty years.

Lines 220-292

Achitophel, in need of a new candidate to make chief of the country, selects David's son Absalom (the Duke of Monmouth) - since there is no one available more fit or warlike. With studied flattery and art, Achitophel begins a long temptation speech to seduce Absalom to the rebellious cause. He informs Absalom that the country anxiously desires him to become king; how long, then, will Absalom deny them?

> **How long wilt thou the general joy detain,**
> **Starve and defraud the people of thy reign?**
> ....
> **Believe me, royal youth, thy fruit must be**
> **Or gathered ripe, or rot upon the tree.**

To augment his argument Achitophel refers to the way in which Absalom's father had to be induced to become king; now, once again, the public is waiting for its future king, Absalom. David is not the same man that he once was: "He is not now, as when on Jorden's sand/The joyful people thronged to see him land." Instead, the king has been weakened by the plot against him: In other words, Charles II has lost popular support ever since the wide promulgation of the "popish plot." Furthermore, the king has no natural allies any more, and Egypt (France), for example, would help Absalom win the throne.

Lines 293-347

Achitophel ends his speech by arguing that Absalom would not only have royal blood, but the complete support of the people; he thus could be a much more powerful ruler than a king by succession (James, for example). Dryden explains how Absalom has been made drunk by flattery and his ambition has been kindled; he has unwarily been "led from virtue's ways./Made drunk with honor, and debauch'd with praise." Then Absalom replies to Achitophel. He defends his father, David, in generous terms. This is Dryden's way of pausing to flatter King Charles II. Absalom asks what right he has to try to wrest the throne away from his father:

> **My father governs with unquestion'd right;**
> **The faith's defender, and mankind's delight;**
> **Good, gracious, just, observant of the laws:**
> **And Heav'n by wonders has espous'd his cause.**

Besides his firm belief that David is a good king, Absalom also feels that his father has been personally good to him; even if it might be right for the people at large to turn against David, certainly he, Absalom, should not:

> The people might assert their liberty;
> But what was right in them were crime in me.
> His favor leaves me nothing to require,
> Prevents my wishes, and outruns desire.
> What more can I expect while David lives?
> All but his kingly diadem he gives.

Lines 348-433

Absalom pauses to point out that the crown, which is all that King David holds back from his son, will rightfully be given to David's brother. Dryden then praises James: "Yet dauntless, and secure of native right,/Of every royal virtue stands possessed." Suddenly, however, Absalom regrets the circumstances of his birth; although he knows he has no legal right to the throne, he still wishes that he had been born higher. At this display of momentary weakness, Achitophel renews his temptation to power. He says that Absalom, unknowingly, has shown that virtue is given to guide a throne; the throne, furthermore, needs someone like Absalom who has a forceful nature. King David, in contrast, has become weak and gives the people more than they need. As Achitophel states of David: "It is true he grants the people all they crave;/And more, perhaps, than subjects ought to have." People should reject a king when he begins to grow weak.

Achitophel assures Absalom that he has carefully weakened the nation's willingness to accept James; "The next successor, whom I fear and hate,/My arts have made obnoxious to the State." If the country will not accept either Charles or James, then it is their right to select their own king; after all, it is better that one man suffer than a whole country. In time, it would be almost inevitable that the people would ask Absalom to be their king. The argument, like all temptations to wrong action, has a logical base.

Lines 434-490

Achitophel continues to argue with Absalom by pointing out that it would be wrong of the king to deny his natural heir and son. Furthermore, James watches Absalom's "progress in the people's hearts" with a great deal of suspicion and envy. When assuming power, James would be obliged to punish Absalom; therefore Absalom should fight for the throne out of self-defense, "nature's eldest law." It is better for Absalom to try his right to the title while the king is still alive than to wait until he had died. Achitophel even suggests that the king, like a lecherous woman, wants the crown to be taken away from him by force because he knows it is not in his province to change the laws of succession. Achitophel's speech appeals to Absalom, who again regrets that he could not have been born somewhere else, where his virtuous qualities might have enabled him to reign naturally. This brings to a close the large second section of the poem: Achitophel's temptation of Absalom.

Lines 491-568

Achitophel begins the next and longest section of the poem which comprises a listing of the support which Absalom would have in the event that there was a struggle for the throne. Achitophel assures Absalom that the various differing parties could be united behind the young challenger. Absalom could gain support, for example, from those who thought the monarch had too much power, as well as from those whose best interests were served when the state was in trouble - pretending to be working for the public good, these work for their own private good. Achitophel lists further groups, and, as the largest of all, the masses of ignorant people: "But far more numerous was the herd of such,/Who think too little, and who talk too much." Dryden asserts that the masses of ignorant people have certain noted leaders who hold high positions throughout the land. Dryden's primary target becomes Zimri, who represents George Villiers, the second Duke of Buckingham. Villiers had never done anything to Dryden, but had managed to annoy him in a variety of ways, primarily by insulting him in his play *The Rehearsal*.

The satirical portrait of Buckingham as Zimri is one of the most memorable parts of the entire poem; Dryden himself was fully aware of the satirical genius in this passage. In his Discourse Concerning **Satire**, for example, Dryden wrote: "The character of Zimri in my Absalom is, in my opinion, worth the whole poem: 't is not bloody, but 't is ridiculous enough; and he for whom it was intended was too witty to resent it as an injury... I avoided the mention of great crimes, and applied myself to the representing of blind sides, and little extravagancies." Dryden, in other words, was as much, if not more, interested in presenting a humorous picture as an injurious one. His portrait of Zimri is delightfully presented; his opening remarks about Zimri are often quoted:

> A man so various, that he seem'd to be
> Not one, but all mankind's epitome:
> Stiff in opinions, always in the wrong;
> Was everything by starts, and nothing long;

Dryden makes particular reference to Buckingham's extravagance: Buckingham had inherited an estate of twenty thousand pounds annually and made no effort to save any of it. As Dryden says:

In squand'ring wealth was his peculiar art:
Nothing went unrewarded but desert.
Beggar'd by fools, whom still he found too late,
He had his jest, and they had his estate.

Zimri quite characteristically enjoyed forming new parties, but he was never made the chief of any of them (which, presumably, is why he kept forming new ones).

Lines 569-629

Dryden continues to satirize his various enemies as he lists the support that Absalom would have if he were to attempt to capture the throne. We hear of Balaam, who represents Theophilus Hastings, the Earl of Huntington; of Calbe, cold because he represents Lord Grey, who reportedly had permitted his wife to have an affair with the Duke of Monmouth; of Nadab, who is William, Lord Howard of Escrick. Dryden then refers to the "rascal rabble" who have no titles or importance; we sense Dryden's strong aristocratic leanings when he writes: "Nor shall the rascal rabble here have place,/Whom kings no titles gave, and God no grace." We recall that Dryden referred to the masses as the "rabble" in some of his earlier poems, notably in *Astraea Redux*. We also hear of Jonas, who represents Sir William Jones, the attorney general who had prosecuted the people arraigned in connection with the "popish plot." He also drew up the Habeas Corpus Act in 1679 - and possibly, the Exclusion Bill backed by the Earl of Shaftesbury. Dryden suggests that Jonas could make treason law - presumably this is Dryden's way of saying, he, too, thinks Jonas authored the Exclusion Bill.

We next hear of Shimei, who represents Slingsby Bethel, one of London's two Whig Sheriffs. Bethel was notorious for packing his juries with Whigs who would vote as he directed and thus enabled him to save those prosecuted by the court party. This poem, we should remember, was written to be presented to the public the week prior to Shaftesbury's trial; however, Shaftesbury was acquitted. Dryden spends considerable time satirizing Shimei. While sheriffs were supposed to be generous, Dryden depicts Shimei (Bethel) as a stingy, miserly, selfish man; thus Shimei, for example, "never broke the Sabbath but for gain," and busied himself in "heaping wealth." Dryden refers to Bethel's court-packing:

> **During his office, treason was no crime;**
> **The sons of Belial had a glorious time;**
> **For Shimei, tho' not prodigal or pelf,**
> **Yet lov'd his wicked neighbor as himself.**

Shimei is further said to enjoy slandering the king:

> **When two or three were gathered to declaim**
> **Against the monarch of Jerusalem,**
> **Shimei was always in the midst of them;**
> **And if they curs'd the king when he was by,**
> **Would rather curse than break good company.**

Dryden then completes his portrait of Shimei by noting that he even used his spare time to write pamphlets against the king.

Lines 630-681

Dryden now treats of Corah, who represents Titus Oates - the man who contrived and related the "popish plot." Oates had originally taken orders in the Church of England, but being disgraced for bad conduct, he subsequently became Catholic. Oates' account of the Jesuit plan to murder the king was thought to be fictitious, and Dryden spends considerable time on this idea. We are first reminded that Titus Oates was the son of a family of ribbon weavers. But soon Dryden begins to discuss Oates' fictitious story at the trial:

> His memory, miraculously great,
> Could plots, exceeding man's belief, repeat;
> ....
> Some future truths are mingled in his book;
> But where the witness fail'd, the prophet spoke.

Dryden then goes on to mention the murder of Agag, representing Sir Edmund Godfrey, the presiding magistrate at Oates' trial who was found, shortly after the trial, lying dead in a field. Oates had thereupon claimed that Godfrey had been murdered by Catholics, thus substantiating his original testimony. Dryden, in contrast, is positing the possibility that Oates himself had killed the judge in order to gain support.

Lines 682-752

Dryden describes Absalom as he makes a series of political tours around the countryside in the hope of winning popular approval. (Historically, Monmouth had, at Shaftesbury's urging, taken such a series of tours.) Absalom makes a political speech claiming that his father has grown old and weak, and that Egypt and Tyrus (France and Holland) have robbed England of her trade. Absalom belittles his father directly for the first time in the poem:

> My father, whom with reverence yet I name,
> Charm'd into ease, is careless of his fame;
> And, brib'd with petty sums of foreign gold,
> Is grown in Bathsheba's embraces old;
> Exalts his enemies, his friends destroys;
> And all his pow'r against himself employs.

The reference to Bathsheba is to the Duchess of Portsmouth, the current mistress of Charles II. Absalom concludes by saying that his father is the sole reason for Israel's dissatisfaction and that he hopes the next successor will give the people less cause for grievance.

His speech ended, we hear of Absalom's popular acclaim:

> The crowd, that still believes their kings oppress,
> With lifted hands their young Messiah bless
> ....
> Fame runs before him as the morning star,
> And shouts of joy salute him from afar.

Dryden refers briefly to "Wise Issachar," who represents Thomas Thynne of Wiltshire, one of Monmouth's hosts on his recent tour through the kingdom. Dryden is being playful when he uses the word "wise," for the Bible tells us that Issachar was "a strong ass couching down between two burdens" (Genesis, xlix, 14). Dryden summarizes some of the other arguments which Absalom uses to win over the people, and refers as well to the charge of Oates that both the king's brother, James, and the king's wife, Queen Catherine, were involved in the "popish plot."

Lines 753-810

Dryden begins one of his many large statements about the laws of kingship. Dryden's central belief, which strongly colors the poem, is that kings are only the custodians of the peoples' will. Kings derive their power from the people and thus, in a sense, are servants as well as served; as Dryden states, "Then kings are slaves to those whom they command,/And tenants to their people's pleasure stand." The king, in short, makes a covenant with the people, in order that everyone will not be free to act as he likes. The contemporary philosopher, Thomas Hobbes, thought that the people did not have the right to break such a covenant, but Dryden wants to establish his belief that in certain cases, it is all right for the people to break the covenant, remove the existing king, and then create a new king. This can be accomplished in certain instances, without being considered a state of anarchy where "all have right to all." A country cannot be expected to tolerate a bad king.

Dryden has now given an account of the various supporters Absalom has in his hopes of opposing the king. It is time for Dryden to survey the country and see what support the king would have to resist Absalom's rebellion.

Lines 811-863

Dryden begins by asking, "Now what relief can righteous David bring?" Because the king has few friends, his allies must be those who dislike the masses of people and would therefore enjoy extinguishing the flames of a popularist revolt. Dryden begins with Barzillai. He represents the Duke of Ormond, who had not only fought bravely for Charles I, but had been a companion of Charles II in his exile. Dryden is filled with praise for Barzillai; we hear of how "In exile with his godlike prince he mourn'd;/For him he suffer'd, and with him return'd." In passing, we should notice this suggestion that the king is God; before, we were also told that Absalom was the new messiah. In any case, Dryden now says hyperbolically of Ormond: "Large was his wealth, but larger was his heart." Dryden gives a brief account of Ormond's large family; six of Ormond's eight sons were dead when the poem was written. The "eldest hope" apparently refers to Thomas, Earl of Ossory, who had been a brave naval fighter, but had died tragically of fever in 1680. Dryden then tries to think of someone else who would help the king.

Lines 864-916

He now introduces "Zadoc the priest," who represents William Sancroft, the Archbishop of Canterbury; and the "Sagan of Jerusalem"--the Bishop of London, Henry Compton. Next we hear of "Him of the Western Dome," representing John Dolben, the Dean of Westminster. "The prophet's sons" would thus be the Westminster schoolboys. (We recall that Dryden had gone to Westminster.) This leads Dryden to remark that colleges depend on kings; thus students "To learning and to loyalty were bred."

Dryden then introduces a "train of loyal peers" who would support the king. We hear first of Adriel, representing the Earl of Mulgrave, whom Dryden made his patron for his AurengZebe, a tragedy published in 1676; thus Mulgrave here is a "Muse's friend." Next comes Jotham - George Saville, the Marquis of Halifax, who tried to mediate between the opposing Whigs and Tories; Saville had long been a loyal servant of Charles II. Then comes Hushai, "the friend of David in distress," who is Laurence Hyde, the Earl of Rochester, one of the foremost ministers in Charles' government. Hushai in the Bible was of great help in crushing Achitophel. Dryden finally asks that his muse allow him to present one more character, Amiel: this is Edward Seymour, recently the Speaker of the House of Commons. Thus Dryden notes that Amiel ruled the Sanhedrin for a long time and "dextrous was he in the crown's defense." Dryden summarizes this group of the king's supporters:

> **These were the chief, a small but faithful band**
> **Of worthies, in the breach who dar'd to stand,**
> **And tempt th'united fury of the land.**

Lines 917-1031

The king's band of loyal followers warn him that Absalom, as a tool of Achitophel, wants to overthrow David. But the King is not to be so easily moved. In a long final speech, the King asserts his own authority in particular and the authority of kings in general:

> **Kings are the public pillars of the State,**
> **Born to sustain and prop the nation's weight;**
> **If my young Samson will pretend a call**
> **To shake the column, let him share the fall.**

In other words, King David argues that if Absalom attempts to destroy David and his government, he will also destroy himself in the process. The king of course would prefer not to have to exhibit his strength: Parents like to forgive their children, and David is no exception. The king laments the fact that his son could not have been born to empire and does not have a kingdom to rule. There is a mixture of compassion for his son and a triumphant claim of invincibility.

David has a great respect for Absalom, but he has an even greater respect for the law. As he states: "The law shall direct my peaceful sway,/And the same law teach rebels to obey." And again, "Law they require, let Law then shew her face;/They could not be content to look on grace." In fact, the king's very last words assert the authority of the law: "For lawful pow'r is still superior found;/When long driv'n back, at length it stands the ground." In short, he will be pushed no further; he will not allow anyone to continue to antagonize him. At this point, God in Heaven makes the skies thunder, and the intended rebellion is dissolved as the people recognize the king's unquestionable power and authority. The poem thus ends with an appropriate assertion of the power of King Charles II.

Comment And Analysis: *Absalom and Achitophel* **can be read in a variety of ways. The reader may place the emphasis on the political parallels between the Biblical account and Dryden's contemporary situation; on the wonderful satirical portraits of characters as different as Zimri and Shimei; or simply on the story as a story.**

One way in which to read *Absalom and Achitophel* **is a symbolic struggle between good and evil, or between Christ and Satan. We recall Dryden's attempts in earlier**

poems to make the hero messianic. Now we have the suggestion that Absalom is Christ, Achitophel is Satan, and King David, God the Father. As kings were believed to derive their authority from God, the last of these equations is not particularly unusual. But as Absalom seems devoid of the common Christian attributes, it seems bizarre that - on one level of the poem's meaning - he should represent Christ. On the other hand, probably the most interesting part of *Absalom and Achitophel* is the second section of the poem which is devoted to Achitophel's temptation of Absalom or, in the allegorical sense, Satan's temptation of Christ. In Milton's poems (at this point well-placed in the public mind), the temptation scenes have great evocative power; the temptation of The Lady by Comus is one of the most memorable of all temptation arguments. In Paradise Regained, Satan's temptation of Christ is magnificently presented. In general, temptation scenes are almost always satisfying, because we usually have an intensified combination of wit and logic being presented more incisively than in other parts of the poem. The long temptation of Absalom is delicately handled at every turn and justifies the very idea of having Absalom symbolize Christ.

One interesting fact about the "satire" in *Absalom and Achitophel* is that this aspect is primarily reserved for the minor characters. It is difficult to think of the entire poem as an extended satire when the Earl of Shaftesbury is hardly satirized at all, particularly when compared to the sketch of Zimri. Shaftesbury's function and presentation in the poem are more demonic than comic, more Satanic than satirical. *Absalom and Achitophel* is a poem in which Dryden "also" treats of his enemies; but first, it is a clever exploitation of a parallel between a Biblical and a contemporary situation. Because the Biblical story is a "given" tradition, the burden of argument did not rest with Dryden. The source immediately enlarged rather than limited the possibilities of Dryden's narrative (as witness the sometimes seemingly endless introduction of further names).

Because *Absalom and Achitophel* is a Biblical allegory with satirical sections, it seems at times to assume the dimensions of a morality play, and perhaps even of a masque. The morality-play aspect of the poem is suggested by the pervasive simplistic contest between good and evil. The final authoritarian speech of King David, furthermore, concludes the play on a richly triumphant note. As a conventional juxtaposition of good and evil, triumphant good forgives conquered evil as Absalom resumes his assigned position in the universe; he was not born to reign and therefore he must not try to. The entire motif of Absalom's heroic rebellion against a father figure, in general, and his actual father, in particular, lends a sense of action and contest to Absalom and Achitophel. Although the mixture of rebellion and temptation directs us to Milton's Paradise Lost, we then realize that it is, however, only a certain atmosphere which Absalom and Achitophel shares with all morality plays.

Perhaps the major accomplishment of the poem is that it changes our attitude toward the king. In the opening of the poem, we see the king in the humorous light of master fornicator and perpetuator of illegitimate children. But this side of Dryden's presentation is a way of both humanizing Charles and of preparing the reader for the introduction of one particular illegitimate child, the Duke of Monmouth. As we work through the various positive and negative feelings expressed about the king, we are undecided as to whether he is actually growing old and weak in the arms of Bathsheba, or whether there is a hidden strength behind his generous nature. The conclusion of the poem of course asserts once and for all that the king is not only strong and stable, but the only bar to the potential chaos in the nation.

King Charles had asked Dryden to write the poem; Dryden has glorified King Charles. Through the defeat of Absalom, Dryden symbolically crushes King Charles' Republican, rebellion-oriented critics. King Charles' enemies are presented in such a negative way that their presence in the poem heightens the reader's sympathy for Charles.

Form And Style: By the time Dryden wrote *Absalom and Achitophel*, he had already completed some dozen poems, numerous plays with delicately written prologues and epilogues, over a dozen critical essays, and some translations from Ovid. In other words, Dryden was already a professional poet when he answered the king's request to write *Absalom and Achitophel*. Dryden's use of the couplet is thus by now masterful. There are of course occasional triplets, presented to prevent the couplets from becoming too monotonous; for example, we can notice the triplet in the opening description of Achitophel:

A fiery soul, which, working out its way,
Fretted the pigmy body to decay,
And o'er-informed the tenement of clay (lines 156-8).

The structure of *Absalom and Achitophel* is basically a division into five parts: (1) the overall explanation of the political situation which establishes firmly the various parallels between Israel and England; (2) the temptation of Absalom by Achitophel; (3) a review of the potential support of Absalom; (4) a review of the potential support of David; (5) David's final speech, asserting his own authority in particular and the authority of kings in general. Of the five sections, the second is the most enjoyable; the third and fourth allow Dryden to exercise his satiric wrath on his enemies; and the fifth, to solidify his political sentiments.

It is important to realize that *Absalom and Achitophel* is a poem of mixed styles, reflecting the mixture of approaches to his material that Dryden used. We have classical, heroic passages; argumentative passages of high rhetorical flourish; small and large satirical sketches; diatribes on political injustice; and digressions on an endless variety of subjects. *Absalom and Achitophel* is, in one sense, a stylistic hall of exhibition in which Dryden can perform endless experiments. In other words, *Absalom and Achitophel* is a stylistic "tour de force." There are great passages of oratory, particularly King David's final speech, and passages of skillful rhetoric, seen most lucidly in Achitophel's repeated temptations of Absalom.

To say that *Absalom and Achitophel* is a stylistic tour de force is not to suggest that there is anything lustreless about Dryden's use of the heroic couplet. (In fact, his skill in handling this unit of poetry seems to have increased as he wrote the poem.) Each couplet crystallizes a particular thought in a clever rhyme: "Kings are the public pillars of the State,/Born to sustain and prop the nation's weight"; "Shimei, whose youth did early promise bring,/Of zeal to God and hatred to his king"; and then there is the wonderful couplet capturing Dryden's feelings about Villiers (Zimri): "A man so various, that he seem'd to be/Not one, but all mankind's epitome." And of Titus Oates' account: "Not weigh'd or winnow'd by the multitude;/But swallowed in the mass, unchew'd and crude." And the wonderful suggestion of David's allies: "Friends he has few, so high the madness grows;/Who dare be such, must be the people's foes." Again and again, Dryden's carefully phrased couplets demand quotation. Dryden loved order, precision and, like King David, proportion: "He knew it was the proper work of kings,/To keep proportion, ev'n in smallest things."

ESSAY QUESTIONS AND ANSWERS

Question: What is Dryden's political philosophy with regard to the right of kings?

Answer: Dryden, like Hobbes, believed that kings derived their power on the one hand from God, but most importantly from a covenant they made with the people: A king is allowed to rule as long as he fulfills the people's needs. When a king is irresponsible and refuses to carry out the popular will, he may have his power revoked. On this point, Dryden disagreed with Hobbes, who felt that once a covenant was made, it could not be broken. Dryden would not have a story to tell, however, if it were not even possible for the people to demand a change of leader. After all, *Absalom and Achitophel* is a poem about the intended usurpation of the throne; Monmouth is described as trying to wrest power away from Charles. Dryden seems to argue that under certain circumstances, the people may revoke their covenant. This is the message of Absalom's long speech in the middle of his political tour. The poem ends, however, with a forceful assertion that the king cannot be challenged by the people. And there are various comments here, as in *Astraea Redux*, which reveal Dryden's general lack of sympathy for the masses of common people. This attitude serves to strengthen his position on the king's inviolable rights. Dryden has successfully supported limited constitutional monarchy.

Question: Is Dryden's suggestion of a further Christian symbolism in *Absalom and Achitophel* successful?

Answer: No, Dryden has not been able to make strong correlations between Achitophel and Satan or between Absalom and Christ. While it is possible to accept the conventional association between the King and God, it is difficult to accept the other two parallels. Dryden's basic Biblical allegory is effective; there is an appropriate character or institution for each of those in England that he wants to depict. But to load the additional religious **metaphor** onto the poem seems to be a weak effort. There is no more than an artificial similarity between Absalom and Christ; furthermore, it would be wrong to have Satan and Christ rebelling together against God. Probably, the basic metaphorical situation came to Dryden's mind as he began to write the temptation scene. Fortunately, he was smart enough not to explore the situation very far; given the characters and the intended rebellion, it would have been illogical to make a strong argument that Absalom represented Christ. We should simply say that the king is to a certain extent God-like, but he is not

God Himself; after his final speech, for example, David watches while God makes the sky fill with thunder; David himself does not bring this tempest about. In the same way, Achitophel may be considered Satanic, but not as representative of Satan. The further religious **metaphor**, in other words, must be limited in its interpretation and assigned a secondary importance in the understanding of the poem.

THE MEDAL

Introduction

In March, 1682, only four months after presenting *Absalom and Achitophel*, Dryden published a second **satire**, entitled *The Medal*. Dryden once again is found attacking his enemy the Earl of Shaftesbury. In the interim not only had Shaftesbury been acquitted of the charge of treason (made because he tried to incite the Duke of Monmouth to wrest the throne from Charles), but he had been glorified by the Whigs in a commemorative medal designed and printed in his honor. Shaftesbury's profile and title adorned one side of the medal; on the other there was a picture of the London skyline, with the famous Tower of London where the Earl had been imprisoned. The medal also had printed on it the date of the Earl's release, November 24, 1681. According to rumors which have persisted over the years, Dryden was inspired to write *The Medal* when King Charles II said to him, "if I was a poet, and I think I am poor enough to be one, I would write a poem on such a subject in the following manner," whereupon he outlined the plan for the poem which Dryden did in fact write.

Dryden wrote an extremely humorous introductory letter to *The Medal*. He dedicated his poem to the Whigs, and referred to the medal itself by saying, "This must needs be a grateful undertaking to your whole party; especially to those who have not been so happy to purchase the original." Then he goes on to suggest a different location for Shaftesbury's head on the medal: "Truth is, you might have spar'd one side of your Medal: the head would be seen to more advantage if it were plac'd on a spike of the Tower." He discusses a three-part tract entitled *No Protestant Plot* believed to have been written by the Earl of Shaftesbury. The tract defended Shaftesbury and the Whigs from having any evil wishes about the fate of the king.

SUMMARY

Lines 1-52

Dryden begins by discussing the city's preoccupation with the medal which had so recently been made. In the poem, the word "Polish," which appears several times, refers to the contemporary joke that Shaftesbury, ever anxious for power, had wanted to be the king of Poland when the throne was temporarily vacated in 1673-4. Dryden then suggests that Shaftesbury, like the medal, is bright on the outside, though base inside: "So like the man; so golden to the sight,/ So base within, so counterfeit and light." Dryden satirically furthers that although it took God only one day to create Adam, it took the medal-maker, Bower, five days to create Shaftesbury (in the medal). The humorous though savage account of Shaftesbury continues as Dryden describes him, for example, as "A beardless chief, a rebel ere a man: /(So young his hatred to his prince began)." In actuality, however, Shaftesbury did not become a rebel until he was twenty-three. Dryden points out Shaftesbury's frustrated desire for power: "Pow'r was his aim; but, thrown from that pretense,/The wretch turn'd loyal in his own defense." This is a reference to the way in which Shaftesbury had deserted Cromwell's government when he was not rewarded for his service.

Lines 53-102

Dryden continues to explain how Shaftesbury disliked serving: "He had a grudging still to be a knave... And rather would be great by wicked means." Shaftesbury, Dryden suggests, was, in effect, a traitor to England: He generally gave weak advice and artfully betrayed the national safety; when unable to earn approval and promotion from the crown, Shaftesbury always tries to prod the people of England into a widespread state of dissatisfaction with the king. As when he was represented by Achitophel, Shaftesbury is once again seen as Satan (this is suggested earlier in the poem by "Lucifer"); as Satan, he is once again rebelling against God while seducing the people toward a rejection of the monarch:

> **When his just sovereign, by no impious way,**
> **Could be seduced to arbitrary sway;**
> **Forsaken of that hope, he shifts the sail,**
> **Drives down the current with a pop'lar gale;**
> **And shews the fiend confess'd without a veil.**
> **He preaches to the crowd that pow'r is lent,**
> **But not convey'd to kingly government.**

As in *Astraea Redux* and *Absalom and Achitophel*, Dryden does not try to conceal his antipathy for the common masses; he discusses their awkward misunderstanding of power and the ease with which they can be swayed; Dryden then remarks sarcastically, "Some think the fools were most, as times went then;/But now the world's o'erstocked with prudent men."

Lines 103-166

Dryden continues to criticize the fickle crowd, noting how difficult it is to know how long any one government or religion will endure. He reiterates the feelings expressed in *Absalom and Achitophel* that England may, in her mad pursuit of excessive liberty, induce anarchy: "Too happy England, if our good we knew,/Would we possess the freedom we pursue!" But the way in which the English people are not satisfied illustrates a defect in man:

> **Ah, what is man, when his own wish prevails!**
> **How rash, how swift to plunge himself in ill;**
> **Proud of his pow'r, and boundless in his will!**

Dryden incorporates a discussion of the jury which had tried and acquitted Shaftesbury. He points out, as he had in *Absalom and Achitophel*, that the members of that jury would be Whigs who, like bloodsucking leeches, voted as directed. These members of that jury foreswore justice and religion; they were irreligious - "Thy rack ev'n scripture to confess their cause" - and irresponsible to the law.

Lines 167-231

Dryden suddenly addresses himself to London in particular, explaining the parallel between the Thames and the Nile rivers. London has wealth which is spread over the land, but as the tide ebbs, it leaves behind monsters in the slime who become seditious. Dryden again disparages the common people, saying "None are so busy as the fool and knave. / Those let me curse." Dryden explains that the common people are primarily concerned with their shops and their customers (we recall the similar thought in the description of the London fire in *Annus Mirabilis*). We then hear of the "trait'rous combination" which refers to the Association to Protect the Protestant Religion and to Aid the King. This was an association planned on papers found among Shaftesbury's possessions, which were used successfully in his defense when he was tried for treason. Dryden has become impatient with the Whig denials of the charges that they had planned treason against the king. And the more they deny, the more accuracy they impart to what they deny: "By proving theirs no plot, they prove 't is worse." Such treason still exists and there are those who willfully would destroy King Charles II and slowly wrest power away from him; they would clip the ring of his crown (damage it), thus preventing him from acting. Dryden's summary of the traitors' desires is harshly invective:

> **For from pretended grievances they rise,**
> **First to dislike, and after to despise;**
> **Then, Cyclop-like, in human flesh to deal,**
> **Chop up a minister at every meal;**
> **Perhaps not wholly to melt down the king,**
> **But clip his regal rights within the ring;**
> **From thence t'assume the pow'r of peace and war;**
> **And ease him by degrees of public care.**

Lines 232-272

Dryden again refers to those who anxiously stand prepared to remove the king from the throne. Then Dryden asserts that republics simply will not grow in some soils and that England is lucky to have a monarchy; as suggested in the previous poems, Dryden usually favors a government based on limited monarchy rather than on a republic. He refers harshly to Shaftesbury: "But thou, the pander of the people's hearts,/(O crooked soul, and serpentine in arts!)." Dryden adds that Shaftesbury's name will be cursed by succeeding generations. Then Shaftesbury is described as a "formidable cripple," one of many references to Shaftesbury's physical infirmities. In any case, the dominant image of Shaftesbury is that of a poisonous venom which infects the nation's brains.

Lines 273-322

Dryden now presents one of the most satirical passages in the poem. He reflects that even if Shaftesbury were successful, his friends would turn against him when they realized that his God was not the same as theirs. Dryden's portrait of Shaftesbury's God is biting and harsh:

> **Thy God and theirs will never long agree;**
> **For thine (if thou hast any) must be one**
> **That lets the world and humankind alone;**
> **A jolly god, that passes hours too well**
> **To promise heav'n, or threaten us with hell.**

The result would be to have a heaven similar to Bedlam, the common name for a particular London insane asylum, the Hospital of St. Mary of Bethlehem. After imagining the kind of god and heaven that would result, he pictures what England would be like if Shaftesbury were to succeed. "If true succession from our isle should fail," Dryden asserts, the country would be involved in an endless series of civil wars. Factions would breed factions, resulting in widespread anarchy; everyone would dislike everyone: "Lords envy lords, and friends with every friend/About their impious merit shall contend." The factions would keep the country in a state of continuous flux until eventually the government might be restored peacefully to the government of a monarch:

> **Thus inborn broils the factions would ingage,**
> **Or wars of exil'd heirs, or foreign rage,**
> **Till halting vengeance overtook our age;**
> **And our wild labors wearied into rest,**
> **Reclin'd us on a rightful monarch's breast.**

Dryden attaches a final Latin quotation (from Ovid) which humorously leaves his subject Shaftesbury more or less helpless; in effect, the quotation means, "it is shameful that these remarks can be made about you and cannot be refuted."

Comment And Analysis: The poem's most fundamental achievement is the rather substantial picture of Dryden's foremost enemy, the Earl of Shaftesbury. He was physically deformed; in his youth he had fought first for Charles I and then for the Parliamentary side in the Civil War. He had been an advisor to Oliver Cromwell, but had failed to achieve great heights in Cromwell's government. When he later helped bring about the Restoration of Charles II, he was made a baron and then an earl. Eventually, however, Shaftesbury became a leader of the opposition against not only Charles but, Dryden assures us, against the idea of monarchy as well.

Dryden is unrelenting in his attack on Shaftesbury and some historians feel that he did Shaftesbury irreparable injustice. For Shaftesbury had, after all, made great contributions to England. It may be that Dryden as an opportunist resented the presence of another opportunist.

The Medal should of course be read against the background of *Absalom and Achitophel*. The treatment of Shaftesbury in both poems makes them two sides of the same coin; however, *The Medal* is generally considered a less outstanding and imaginative poem than *Absalom and Achitophel*. There are of course exceptionally brilliant parts in *The Medal*. One is Dryden's satirical sketch of the way in which each of the London dissenters interprets the Scripture according to his own mood and feelings; another is the savage picture of Shaftesbury's jolly god who has no time to become involved with the ideas of heaven and hell. But such bits and pieces do not necessarily add up to a poem which is brilliant throughout.

Form And Style: Unlike *Absalom and Achitophel*, *The Medal* cannot be divided into separate sections. The poem is generally organized in a chronological way, proceeding through the events of Shaftesbury's career. But the poem is again an "occasional" piece, inspired by and designed to describe the issuing of the commemorative medal in Shaftesbury's honor. The mood of satire is sustained throughout, but with varying intensity; that is, from the point of view of style, the poem is "uneven." Parts are very good, parts are boring and rather trite. To a certain extent, the same is true of *Absalom and Achitophel*.

> But because *The Medal* is only one third as long as the earlier satire, the reader is inclined to be less tolerant of weakness. Dryden continues to write in heroic couplets and introduces thirteen triplets for variation. There is some parenthetical comment, as well as quite an amount of alliteration.

ESSAY QUESTIONS AND ANSWERS

Question: What is the importance of Dryden's second **satire**, *The Medal?*

Answer: The poem is important primarily as an extension of Dryden's satirical attack on the Earl of Shaftesbury, begun in the earlier satire *Absalom and Achitophel.* Once again there is a harsh cynical treatment of Shaftesbury. The poem is also important because it shows Dryden's distrust and dislike for the people at large, the common citizenry. Both now and in earlier poems, Dryden makes it perfectly clear that he believes England needs to be ruled by a monarch rather than by a Republican group of leaders who would represent the rabble; this is why he writes:

> For in some soil republics will not grow:
> Our temp'rate isle will no extremes sustain
> Of pop'lar sway or arbitrary reign,
> But slides between them both into the best,
> Secure in freedom, in a monarch blest.

And the very last lines of the poem repeat the idea of looking forward to resting securely under the leadership of a monarch. Dryden of course was writing the poem for the purposes of belittling the king's enemy, Shaftesbury, and thus we would expect the element of praise for the king; but nevertheless, we must take these panegyrics as indicative of Dryden's political sentiments.

Question: Is the **satire** in *The Medal* as delicately conceived as the **satire** in *Absalom and Achitophel?*

Answer: No. Dryden's second **satire** is neither as imaginative nor as comprehensive as his first. In *Absalom and Achitophel* there are striking satirical portraits of his enemies, like that of Zimri. But in *The Medal*, which is in effect an extended portrait of Shaftesbury, the **satire** never reaches the heights (or depths, depending on one's point of view) that it does in the earlier poem. The **satire** functions throughout *The Medal* in a rather insulting and sometimes merely pejorative way, without real basis for insult; the **satire** is trying to attach itself to a subject - the commemorative medal - which is not large enough to be given a universal importance, in contrast to the planned rebellion in *Absalom and Achitophel*.

MAC FLECKNOE

Introduction

Mac Flecknoe is usually considered to be one of Dryden's best poems. Apparently written in 1678, it was read only privately until it was published in 1682 - even then, without Dryden's permission. It was first "officially" published in 1684, when Dryden allowed it to be included in Jacob Tonson's anthology, *Miscellany Poems*. Dryden's earlier **satire** *The Medal* had been replied to by Thomas Shadwell in his *Medal of John Bayes*, which maliciously attacked Dryden. It was more savage than either *The Medal* or *Mac Flecknoe*. In any case, in *Mac Flecknoe* Dryden replied to Shadwell effectively, with great humor and only slight contempt.

Mac Flecknoe, generally rated as Dryden's best short **satire**, makes Thomas Shadwell its central target. Shadwell, in addition to being the author of *The Medal of John Bayes*, was a Restoration dramatist of only questionable talent, who had smugly supposed himself to be the next great dramatist to follow Ben Jonson. For this reason, and for his attack on Dryden, *Mac Flecknoe* was written. Another less conspicuous reason was that in 1678, Shadwell had openly praised Buckingham's play *The Rehearsal*, which contained an attack on Dryden. Until that time, Dryden and Shadwell had been good friends.

Dryden originally denied that he had written *Mac Flecknoe*, but later he readily confessed his authorship. In his 1692 Discourse concerning Satire, he asked the reader to consider as examples of **satire** a few of his own poems: *Absalom and Achitophel* and *Mac Flecknoe*. It should be noted, in passing, that Shadwell's plays were based on Jonsonian "humors," or outstanding personal foibles. Thus *Mac Flecknoe* contains ample **allusions** to some of the plays which Shadwell wrote, including *Psyche, The Miser, Humorists, The Hypocrite*, and *The Virtuoso*.

The Real Flecknoe

In 1678, Richard Flecknoe, an Irish poet, died. He had, by the time of his death, become synonymous with bad poetry. He was also believed to be a Catholic priest. There was no hostility between Dryden and Flecknoe, and in fact, Flecknoe praised Dryden in his 1670 collection of *Epigrams*, where he wrote, for example, the rather lustreless, unsatisfactory lines. "Dreyden the Muses darling and delight,/ Than whom none ever flew so high a flight." As one further detail, we can note that the poet Andrew Marvell saw him in Rome in about 1645 and recorded the meeting in his satire, *Flecknoe, An English Priest At Rome.*

Flecknoe had been considered a very bad poet. For this reason Dryden chose to have him confer his empire, or crown, symbolizing bad writing, on Thomas Shadwell. Instead of following in the tradition of Ben Jonson's excellent poetry, Shadwell should instead carry on the tradition of the notoriously poor poetry of Flecknoe; he would be the son of (Mac) Flecknoe. Aside from his being a bad poet, Flecknoe was Irish, and in Dryden's day, this in itself was something to ridicule; the Irish were mistakenly but humorously considered uncultured boors. In any case, there was no real relationship between Flecknoe and Shadwell. The relationship is, rather, invented as a convenient vehicle for Dryden's satirical counterattack on Shadwell.

There is a satirical use of Christian religion in the poem. Shadwell is sometimes depicted as Christ, while Flecknoe, who "baptizes" Shadwell as the next bad poet, is referred to as John the Baptist. Heywood and Shirley, inferior Elizabethan dramatists, are also brought in as Old Testament characters. As a parallel to the John the Baptist-Christ metaphorical framework, we have Flecknoe appearing as an emperor choosing a successor, Shadwell. The blending of religion, classicism, myth, fable, etc., makes Mac Flecknoe a delightful reading experience. The alternative title which Dryden gave his **satire** seems appropriate enough: "A Satire Upon The True-Blue-Protestant Poet, T. S."

SUMMARY

Lines 1-42

The poem opens with the introduction of Flecknoe, a monarch like the emperor Augustus, who reigns throughout the realm of nonsense. One of the main satirical modes is the giving of value to everything which the poet considers valueless; for example a pretended praise conferred on forms of superlative ignorance. But Flecknoe has decided, once and for all, to settle the question of succession. This in itself is humorous when we realize that Dryden is now making fun of something about which he had previously written seriously. While looking around for a successor, Flecknoe has decided on Shadwell, who must reign because he alone can approximate the bad poetry written by Flecknoe:

> ..(Flecknoe)
> Cried: "'T is resolv'd; for nature pleads, that he
> Should only rule who most resembles me.
> Sh____ alone my perfect image bears.
> Mature in dulness from his tender years:
> Sh____ alone, of all my sons, is he
> Who stands confirm'd in full stupidity.

Dryden follows a poetic custom of abbreviating the name of his adversary; but "Sh____" is of course Shadwell. (The line scans properly with the two-syllable "Shadwell.") In any case, Flecknoe bequeaths to Shadwell the crown of his dullness.

This is a richly comic concept, and was to be borrowed by Alexander Pope in his *Dunciad*.

Dryden's humor unrolls in laughter as Flecknoe explains further that Shadwell should be his successor, because he has the least meaning in his poetry:

> The rest to some faint meaning make pretense,
> But Sh___ never deviates into sense.
> Some beams of wit on other souls may fall,
> Strike thro', and make a lucid interval;
> But Sh___'s genius night admits no ray,
> His rising fogs prevail upon the day.

To enlarge the idea not only of succession but of a continuing progression from bad to worse poets, Flecknoe briefly refers to the line of succession from the bad Elizabethan dramatists Heywood and Shirley:

> Heywood and Shirley were but types of thee,
> Thou last great poet of tautology.
> Even I, a dunce of more renown than they,
> Was sent before but to prepare thy way.

In *Mac Flecknoe*, vices are virtues; the worst poet possible, one who uses tautologies, for example, must be the successor to the throne of dullness. By comparison with Heywood, Shirley, and even Flecknoe, it must be admitted that Shadwell is the worst of all possible poets and thus "deserves" the crown.

Lines 42-84

Flecknoe continues his discussion of Shadwell by referring to him as "the new Arion." (Arion was an ancient Greek musician who, when threatened by some sailors, asked to play his lyre; he did and then jumped overboard, where dolphins carried him safely to shore.) Dryden also refers to Shadwell's play, *Psyche*. The speech is essentially light and humorous, while at the same time filled with comic **irony**. When Flecknoe has finished, Dryden writes of him: "Here stopp'd the good old sire, and wept for joy/In silent raptures of the hopeful boy." Of Shadwell he says, in a word, "for anointed dulness he was made." Dryden refers to Augusta fears, that is, to the fears of a city where such events as the "popish plot" can occur. He then describes the way in which Flecknoe enters the "Nursery," an actual London theater for boys and girls to study drama, established by a patent issued by Charles II in 1664. Great poets like Fletcher and Jonson cannot enter there, but Simpkin, as representative of bad poets, can easily gain admission. (There had been a collection of farces about a clown named Simpkin.)

Lines 85-117

At this location, Flecknoe designs Shadwell's throne:

> **Here Flecknoe, as a place to fame well known,**
> **Ambitiously desin'd his Sh___'s throne;**
> **For ancient Dekker prophesied long since,**
> **That in this pile should reign a mighty prince,**
> **Bourn for a scourge of wit, and flail of sense.**

Dekker, a dramatist writing under James I, was not considered as bad a poet as Dryden implies here. In any case, Dryden continues by referring to some of Shadwell's plays: *Psyche*, *The Miser* (which was an adaptation of *Moliere's L'Avare*), and the *Humorists*. Once Flecknoe had chosen Shadwell as his successor, Fame began to spread the news, and then a progression began. Instead of carpets, there are piles of the limbs of mangled poets; neglected authors emerge from their dusty shops. Dryden mentions some of the bad poets, introducing Ogleby, a notoriously terrible poet whom both Dryden and Pope satirized. Flecknoe is on the throne with Shadwell, and "lambent dulness play'd around his face." Shadwell then vows to uphold the dullness so successfully maintained by Flecknoe:

> So Sh___ swore, nor should his vow be vain,
> That he till death true dullness would maintain;
> And, in his father's right, and realm's defense,
> Ne'er to have peace with wit, nor truce with sense.

Lines 118-144

Flecknoe, as king, crowns the heir, Shadwell. The king holds in his hand a copy of Love's Kingdom, a weak tragi-comedy by Flecknoe (and the only one of his plays to be performed), from which Dryden humorously suggests the equally weak Shadwell play, Psyche, must have come. Dryden describes Flecknoe as he prepares to speak:

> The sire then shook the honors of his head,
> And from his brows damps of oblivion shed
> Full on the filial dullness...

Flecknoe praises his son and heir, requesting that he be able to rule from Ireland to the Barbadoes (satirical cultural dimensions), and that he be an even greater king than Flecknoe has been (i.e., even duller). When Flecknoe pauses, everyone cries, "Amen."

Lines 145-170

Flecknoe resumes his speech. In one of the high points of the **satire**, Flecknoe counsels Shadwell to advance ignorance:

> ...My son, advance
> Still in new impudence, new ignorance.
> Success let others teach, learn thou from me
> Pangs without birth, and fruitless industry.
> Let Virtuosos in five years be writ;
> Yet not one thought accuse thy toil of wit.

VERSE ESSAYS

RELIGIO LAICI

Introduction

Dryden's *Religio Laici*, meaning "the faith of a layman," was published in November, 1682. Apparently two different editions appeared within the year, but the textual variations are sufficiently minor to enable us to assume that they are probably not Dryden's own changes. In writing a verse essay, Dryden explicitly followed in the tradition of the Latin poet Horace's *Epistles*. After acknowledging Horace (toward the conclusion of a lengthy and somewhat tediously written "Preface" to *Religio Laici*), Dryden points out that "the expressions of a poem design'd purely for instruction ought to be plain and natural, and yet majestic." And this, in effect, is the style which Dryden achieves in *Religio Laici*.

A book of Biblical criticism, Father Simon's *Critical History of the Old Testament*, had appeared and caused immediate controversy in 1678. French officials placed a ban on the book, but enough copies survived for one of Dryden's friends, Henry Dickinson, to translate it from French into English. Its appearance in 1682 was the occasion behind Dryden's writing this verse essay, *Religio Laici*.

What was the explanation behind the controversy? In Dryden's age, there were two possible attitudes one could have toward the Bible: either one considered it the supreme guide in theological matters and representative of the absolute authority of God; or one could consider the Bible a less reliable authority than that claimed by the tradition of the church. While some people thought that the Bible was the final word on all problems, others insisted that the most accurate Christian tradition was instead represented by the Roman Catholic Church. Protestantism, adhering to Scripture, divided into various sects as interpretations differed; Catholicism adhered to its early traditions as the first established Christian Church. Father Simon's idea was to undermine the validity of the Bible; if the Bible could be found erroneous, people would inevitably (he thought) have to embrace the Catholic Church as a last recourse (even if for no other reason). If the Catholic tradition was itself divinely inspired, it had more authority than the Scriptures. As Catholics thus maximized the importance of the Church, Protestants maximized the importance of the Bible. By attacking the Bible, Simon thought he was cleverly defending the Roman Catholic Church; however, considering his book more offensive than defensive, the French authorities had immediately suppressed it.

A third attitude one could hold toward this problem was, in effect, one of compromise: the Church of England, to which Dryden belonged when he wrote *Religio Laici*, accepted with relatively little difficulty the main doctrinal truths as expressed in the Bible, while at the same time acknowledging the authority behind the tradition of the early Catholic Church. This is the position which Dryden adopts at the end of the poem, although he makes some modifications in his emphasis on peace.

A fourth solution (which Dryden did not consider a real solution) to the problem of final authority was the philosophy of deism: rather than posit divine truth in any one particular religion, man should realize that all men, in different ways, try to achieve an understanding of a God and an afterlife. Dryden discusses this position for most of the first half of *Religio Laici*. (He does not consider Father Simon until line 224.) Although Dryden's main interest is in resolving the competition between Scripture and authority of the Church, he feels that the Christian religion in general is the most help. Dryden concedes, however, that heathen (like Socrates) who are of course uninformed of Christian text, can in their own right gain entrance to heaven. In this concession, Dryden was departing from the established views of the Church of England.

SUMMARY

Lines 1-41

Dryden begins his poem by questioning the power of reason. What sort of faculty is reason by comparison with the soul? Reason is a fallible faculty and incapable of reaching God; it has only a "glimmering ray" which is easily eclipsed by the "supernatural light" of religion. How can man expect, in short, to be able to "reason" God correctly? Dryden admits, however, that some, whose lamp of reason shone more brightly than others, have been able to form philosophies explaining God, "that Universal He." Dryden refers to the conventional theological argument that God is the first mover (primum mobile), Himself unmoved. We also hear of Stagarite, representing Aristotle.

In any case, nobody has ever been able to prove or confirm the precise essence of God. And, similarly, no one has been able to discover what chief good man should work for:

> **But least of all could their endeavors find**
> **What most concern'd the good of humankind;**
> **For happiness was never to be found,**
> **But vanish'd from 'em like enchanted ground.**

Dryden then suggests some of the possible things for which man searches, such as contentment, virtue, and pleasure; then he asks his main skeptical question: "How can the less the greater comprehend?/Or finite reason reach infinity?" The reason Dryden can assert this question is that anything that could fathom God would be greater than God. And this, by definition, is impossible.

Lines 42-85

Dryden turns his attention to the deists, who think they have an answer in their belief that "God is that spring of good; supreme and blest;/We, made to serve, and in that service blest." Dryden is disparaging of those who profess to have reasoned out the essence of God; he explains how man, surrounded by earthly injustice, imagines "a future state," a second life "Where God's all-righteous ways will be declar'd." If the bad are all denied entrance to heaven, and everyone who is good is admitted, what need is there of a God? Dryden changes the direction of the argument, charging that what the deists consider the result of their reason is, in fact, only divine revelation:

> These truths are not the product of thy mind,
> But dropp'd from heaven, and of a nobler kind.
> Reveal'd religion first inform'd thy sight,
> And Reason saw not, till Faith sprung the light.

It must be revelation, for truths which were obscure to Aristotle would not now suddenly seem clear. Dryden feels that one cannot know any more by way of reason alone than any of the ancient philosophers like Plutarch, Seneca, and Cicero: "Those giant wits, in happier ages born." It would never have occurred to them to worship one God alone.

Lines 86-133

Dryden continues his discussion of the heathens who, to expiate their sins, offered sheep and oxen in sacrifice; how easy, therefore, Dryden asserts, for a rich man to expiate his sins. Dryden's discussion of atonement for sins continues in a very straightforward manner. There is nothing particularly confusing about Dryden's presentation of theological arguments; he is, after all, writing only as a "layman" and therefore knows that he is not expected to have final answers to traditionally complex problems. He charges the deists for not recompensing their sins; the deists are lost because they never feel remorse: "See then the Deist lost: remorse for vice,/ Not paid; or paid, inadequate in price." Dryden then says that compared to Christianity, all other religions are inadequate.

Lines 134-183

Having suggested that the Bible records examples of God's will, Dryden refers specifically to Father Simon's charges against the Bible; that is, Dryden defends the Bible's validity. After all, he asks, what reason could there be for divinely inspired men to deceive us? Dryden praises the Bible's style as being "majestic and divine." How can reason possibly improve on the divine truths of the Bible?

> **To what can Reason such effects assign,**
> **Transcending nature, but to laws divine?**
> **Which in that sacred volume are contain'd;**
> **Sufficient, clear, and for that use ordain'd.**

Dryden presents the deist objections to the Bible: the Bible, for example, could not possibly contain the truth of a law universally applied "to all, and everywhere." The truth of God's law must apply to those who do not even acknowledge Him; and God's law has "A style so large as not this book can claim." The deist asks, furthermore: Of what use is the Bible to those who were not present and never saw the light?

Lines 184-223

Dryden now turns to the major objection which deists raise against Christianity: namely, no one religion can claim to be the only authentic one because people not educated to the Scripture still believe in God and an afterlife. Dryden here departs from the accepted view of his own Church of England, describing these heathen:

> **They, who the written rule had never known,**
> **Were to themselves both rule and law alone:**
> **To nature's plain indictment they shall plead,**
> **And by their conscience be condemn'd or freed.**

Those who follow the rules of their reason and direct their thoughts to heaven may arrive there as probably as those familiar with the Scripture. Many heathens, like Socrates, will be able to see "their Maker's face."

Lines 224-275

Dryden now refers directly to Father Simon's *Critical History Of The Old Testament* which had been so recently translated and improved by Dryden's young friend Dickinson. Dryden takes a very negative attitude toward the "weighty book," the result of many years of "crabbed toil." He explains how Father Simon has noted all of the problems and inaccuracies involved in the textual transmission of the Scripture down through the ages. Father Simon is considered by some as "not too much a priest," because he has a secret, an unacknowledged ulterior motive for attacking the Bible. Dryden then answers Father Simon's accusations by arguing that if the written word (the Scripture) can be transformed down through the ages, then consider how much more transformed the spoken word (Catholic "tradition") must be:

> If written words from time are not secur'd,
> How can we think have oral sounds endur'd?
> Which thus transmitted, if one mouth has fail'd,
> Immortal lies on ages are intail'd.

Just as Simon had attacked the validity of the Bible by demonstrating the changes, so Dryden is now replying by attacking the validity of the oral tradition by demonstrating its changes.

Lines 276-345

Dryden now presents the opposite argument, the one made by Father Simon: if the original Scripture has been lost, and all subsequent copies disagree how can one turn elsewhere than to the established tradition of the church: "Or Christian faith can have no certain ground,/Or truth in Church tradition must be found." Dryden agrees that it would indeed be nice to have an ideal, uncorrupted church, but since there is not such a church, the tradition is generally more fallible than supposed, and the Scripture is satisfactory:

> **God would not leave mankind without a way;**
> **And that the Scriptures, tho' not everywhere**
> **Free from corruption, or intire, or clear,**
> **Are uncorrupt, sufficient, clear, intire,**
> **In all things which our needful faith require.**

Having asserted that the Scripture is satisfactory, Dryden turns to a reexamination of tradition. He concedes that some tradition is needed; there are many unclear points in the Bible which are cleared up by tradition. To reject all tradition, therefore, would be an act of ignorance:

> **Must all tradition then be set aside?**
> **This to affirm were ignorance or pride.**
> **Are there not many points, some needful sure**
> **To saving faith, that Scripture leaves obscure?**

Dryden is thus continuously working toward a compromise: he is defending the Church of England, which thus involves a defense of both Scripture and tradition.

Dryden repeats his previously stated belief that the unlettered man can gain access to heaven just as easily as the educated Christian; some must study the Scripture and others must be taught; Heaven, after all, is not restricted in its membership to men of wit. Tradition can sometimes give "truth the reverend majesty of age." Tradition does have some authority. Once it had a great deal more, but because tradition is always undergoing slight modification, it comes to represent probability rather than truth: "But since some flaws in long descent may be,/They make no truth, but probability."

Lines 346-403

Tradition has frequently been challenged as, for example, by Arius, a fourth-century heretic who denied the doctrine of the trinity, and by Pelagius who in the fifth century denied the idea of original sin. The stories of their beliefs changed in the telling, and thus Dryden emphasizes again the superiority of the written over the spoken word: "Tradition written therefore more commends/Authority, than what from voice descends." Furthermore, the Catholic (Universal) Church cannot validly claim supreme authority because it represents only a part and not the whole of Christianity; even if the Catholic Church is allowed to hand down the tradition, does that mean it can interpret any more judiciously? The Bible is designed to be used by all sects, not simply by the Catholics. Catholic priests passed through an era in which they thought they had a monopoly on interpretation of the scripture; it became difficult to tell whether they influenced the Bible's direction or whether the Bible influenced theirs; as Dryden summarizes: "At last, a knowing age began t'enquire/ If they the book, or that did them inspire." From the first seeds of deviation arose the larger trend toward individual interpretation: everyone interpreted the Scripture as they chose (and presumably in a way that mitigated sin and guilt):

> **The book thus put in every vulgar hand,**
> **Which each presum'd he best could understand,**
> **The common rule was made the common prey,**
> **And at the mercy of the rabble lay.**

It is interesting that Dryden still is thinking of the public at large as "the rabble"; this, we recall, is the same epithet he employed in both *Astraea Redux* and in *Absalom and Achitophel*.

Lines 404-456

Individual interpretation of the Scripture led to the formation of various sects: "a thousand daily sects rise up and die." Dryden then compromises: Important matters of religion do not lie in small, scholarly details. Both Church and Scripture agree on the larger, vital, and essential points. Dryden says of the fine points: "'T is some relief that points not clearly known/Without much hazard may be let alone." If our reason forces us to disagree with the opinion of the Church, it is preferable to keep our dissent to ourselves than to stir up public controversy; social agitation is too high a price to pay for minute disagreements. For although we may disagree over the fine points of interpretation, we nevertheless agree on having a general peace on earth:

> **That private Reason 't is more just to curb,**
> **Than by disputes the public peace disturb.**

> For points obscure are of small use to learn;
> But common quiet is mankind's concern.

And on this note of peace, Dryden humbly concludes.

Comment And Analysis: Dryden's account of the differences between the authority of the "tradition" of the Roman Catholic Church and the Scripture as competing forces is straightforward. Although he is purportedly writing (as announced by the title) as a layman, it is at once obvious that Dryden has a sound knowledge of the theological points of controversy. It is typical of Dryden, however, as a member of the Church of England, to want to reduce polemics and induce compromise. From Dryden's point of view, the larger questions man can raise are answered in the same way by both the Bible and the traditional interpretation of the Bible made by the early Roman Catholic Church. It is much better to keep one's private objections to small doctrinal disputes to oneself; the public peace achieved is more than worth the muffled dissatisfaction. This is typical of Dryden's conservative political feelings; an orderly society is an ideal goal.

There are two basic ways one can read *Religio Laici*. The emphasis can be placed on the theological debate or on the poetry. The poem, for example, could just as easily have been rendered in prose: in fact, Dryden's lines are simply conventional divisions into rhyming units. On the one hand, the importance of the poem is its attempt to answer the deists, to answer Father Simon, and to evolve a synthesis between conflicting Scripture and Church. As a result, the poem can be read as an elaborate and skillful defense of the position taken, for the most part, by the Church of England.

On the other hand, some of the theological arguments are outworn or boring; from a theological point of view, there is very little that is striking or novel in *Religio Laici*. True, the poem presents current problems, but it offers no new solutions. The value of the poem lies therefore in its poetic harmony, its rhythmical lines, and its highly articulate and rhetorical summaries of arguments and counter-arguments. In other words, some readers choose to concentrate on religion and others on poetry when approaching *Religio Laici*. Dryden's title, we should recall, was followed by the phrase "A Poem." That is, he realized that he was writing an artistic "poem," at the same time that he was presenting a statement of his faith as a layman. In any case, Dryden's arguments in *Religio Laici* are poetically fashioned without losing any of their logic. This is a philosophical poem of the highest order, and most critics consider it a successful blend of controversy with poetic statement; of politics with polemics; and of rhetoric with reduction.

Form And Style: The style of *Religio Laici* is basically simple; the language flows evenly throughout without reliance on baroque imagery or artful allusions. There is a minimum of allusion and a maximum of concentration on the essential points which Dryden wants to emphasize. He carefully and systematically replies both to the deists and to Father Simon. And while doing so, Dryden was quite consciously trying to write a verse essay which would read like one of Horace's epistles.

Dryden elaborates on his attempt at this imitation in his preface to *Religio Laici:*

> If anyone be so lamentable a critic as to require the smoothness, the numbers, and the turn of heroic poetry in this poem, I must tell him that, if he has not read Horace, I have studied him, and hope the style of his Epistles is not ill imitated here. The expressions of a poem design'd purely for instruction ought to be plain and natural, and yet majestic.
>
> Dryden's use of words like "smoothness," "plain," and "natural" express and also demonstrate the style of *Religio Laici.* However, in places Dryden's style is more elaborate than he would have us believe; certain passages have rhetorical flourish which is not central to the meaning. But for the most part, Dryden adheres to the Horatian formula of simplicity which he has chosen to use.

ESSAY QUESTIONS AND ANSWERS

Question: Although Dryden thought he was writing *Religio Laici* primarily as a member of the Church of England, is there any evidence that he was already inclined toward Roman Catholicism?

Answer: Yes. There is considerable material in *Religio Laici* which foreshadows the **themes** Dryden would assert later in *The Hind and the Panther.* As Louis Bredvold has explained, both poems are built on a foundation which combines both skepticism and fideism. Even in 1682, Dryden, though perhaps not consciously, was moving toward Roman Catholicism; and if this is true, then Dryden's subsequent conversion can be viewed as a less hypocritical act. Dryden's Preface clearly shows that Dryden himself thought he was writing as a member of the Church of England. However, in the poem Dryden makes both of the conventional fideistic arguments: one beginning with an attack on reason in matters of religion, and the other appealing to the necessity of accepting some authority in the tradition of the Church. Dryden's *Religio Laici* opens quite directly with a concise attack on reason:

Dim as the borrow'd beams of moon and stars

To lonely, wearly wand'ring travelers
Is Reason to the soul: and, as on high
Those rolling fires discover but the sky,
Not light us here, so Reason's glimmering ray
Was lent, not to assure our doubtful way,
But guide us upward to a better day.

Dryden devotes a great deal of time to defending Christianity and "revelation" against the philosophy of deism: He is attacking the authority of reason. Later, in *The Hind and the Panther*, he is attacking the reasoning of the Protestants. In both cases the Christian religion itself is Dryden's primary concern. That his argument in the second poem is against the church to which he belonged when writing the first, should not obscure the similarity of the philosophical content of both poems. Whether consciously or not, Dryden was already moving toward an acceptance of the Catholic religion and toward a recognition of the authority of the tradition and organization of the Church.

Question: If Dryden was attracted to the Roman Catholic church, does *Religio Laici* contain any evidence that Dryden was not satisfied with the Church of England?

Answer: Yes, but the evidence is minimal. There is more of an attraction to Catholicism than a rejection of Anglicanism. Dryden's criticism really takes the form of admitting that the Church of England could be substantially improved; it lacks sufficient belief in either Church authority or Scripture. There is a certain amount of dissatisfaction with the Anglican compromise: this is suggested, for example, when Dryden writes: "Such an Omniscient Church we wish indeed;/'T were worth Both Testaments, and cast in the Creed." We sense Dryden's sincere desire to have authority in matters of religion posited somewhere in particular. He seems to realize that there is something lacking in the Church of England. He will turn to a close and critical examination of Anglicanism in *The Hind and the Panther*.

THE HIND AND THE PANTHER

Introduction

The Hind and the Panther, one of Dryden's most famous poems, was published in the spring of 1687, two years after James II, a Catholic, became the King of England. As discussed previously (see introductory chapter), Dryden converted to Roman Catholicism sometime during 1687, probably very shortly after James succeeded to the throne. It should be noted once again that Dryden's name did not appear on any of the various editions issued in 1687, but even then he was generally assumed to be the author.

James II made it very clear when he began to rule that he had little sympathy for Protestant dissenters. The Test Act of 1673 required all members of Parliament to swear that they did not believe in transubstantiation. The act therefore virtually prevented all Catholics from assuming positions in the English government. James II ignored the act and then, in April 1687, failing to gain the support of any dissenters, he issued a Declaration of Indulgence which gave both Catholics and Dissenters the freedom of worship. *The Hind and the Panther* was designed (particularly part three) to hasten religious toleration. When James' Declaration appeared only one week prior to the date when Dryden's long poem was going to press, he had to attach a preface apologizing for no longer being concerned with a timely subject. In any case, Dryden was satisfied with his poem: He made no attempt to reduce the sections on religious tolerance.

The Hind and the Panther is an allegorical depiction of the friction between various religions in Dryden's time, particularly between the Hind, symbolizing Roman Catholicism, and the Panther, symbolizing the Church of England. Dryden is of course hoping for a reconciliation between these two major religions. Other religious sects allegorically presented in the poem include: the Bear, symbolizing the Independents; the Hare, the Quakers; the Ape, the Atheists or Freethinkers; the Boar, the Baptists; Reynard the fox, the Unitarians; and the Wolves, the Presbyterians. Further symbols are the Lion, representing King James II; and Caledonia, representing England. (Recall the earlier use of Israel in *Absalom and Achitophel*.)

A Poem In Three Parts

Although some readers have criticized Dryden's conversion to Catholicism in 1685, we must remember that he remained loyal to the Catholic Church until his death; because of this loyalty, Dryden was later denied various positions which would have been his. In any case, in *The Hind and the Panther*, Dryden is attempting both to explain and to justify his conversion from the Church of England to Catholicism. Further titled by Dryden, "A Poem in Three Parts," *The Hind and the Panther* moves slowly through three increasingly longer sections: In the first section, Dryden presents all of the allegorical characters with an account of the different problems posed by each of the religious groups represented; in the second part, we have a long dialogue between the Hind and the Panther which systematically covers the primary religious and theological arguments of Dryden's time, many of which were already examined in *Religio Laici*; finally, in the very long third part, England's particular polemics are discussed through the use first of the fable of the Swallows (who represent the English), and then through the fable of the Buzzard (Bishop Burnet).

Dryden's presentation of an allegorical debate between the Hind and the Panther has been widely parodied, beginning most notably with the now-famous 1687 spoof, *The Hind and the Panther Transvers'd to the Story of the Country-Mouse and the City-Mouse*, written by Charles Montague, Earl of Halifax, and Matthew Prior. Perhaps because of its parodies, perhaps because of its length, *The Hind and the Panther* has been substantially reduced in most anthologized versions of the poem. One should bear in mind that some parts are more important than others; the summary which follows has tried to devote more time to the important points.

PART I: SUMMARY

Lines 1-103

Dryden begins with what has now become a famous and often-quoted depiction of the Hind, the Catholic Church:

A milk-white Hind, immortal and unchang'd,
Fed on the lawns, and in the forest rang'd;
Without unspotted, innocent within,
She fear'd no danger, for she knew no sin.

Dryden refers, allegorically, to the way in which the Hind has been pursued and to some of her "martyr'd offspring," representing the various Catholic priests who had been executed in England since the Reformation. We are introduced to the "bloody Bear, an Independent beast," which represents the Independents, a religious group that rejected all traditional ritual and made the concept of the congregation central. Next comes the "Quaking Hare" that "Profess'd neutrality, but would not swear," referring to the Quakers who rejected outright the taking of any oath; then "the buffoon Ape," symbolizing the Freethinkers, or Atheists; next arrives the Lion, James II; the Boar, representing the Anabaptists (the Baptists, derived from a German religious sect, were persecuted extensively in England); and Reynard the fox, the Unitarians. Each faction or sect is presented in an economy of words; Dryden does not yet dwell on the faults of each. All of these non-Catholic groups rely too extensively on reason in matters of religion. Thus we move suddenly into an extended rumination regarding the respective capabilities of reason and faith; as in the crisp opening of *Religio Laici*, Dryden belittles the possibility of knowing God through the human faculty of reason; revelation is not needed when man can perceive naturally. Because revelation is needed to know God, He cannot be known in any other way (as, for example, through the senses).

Lines 104-211

Dryden slowly expands his discussion of the supremacy of faith over reason, beginning with the comment: "Let Reason then at her own quarry fly,/But how can finite grasp infinity?" Dryden explains how God revealed miracles to man in order that man would realize that there was something for him outside the realms of sense and reason:

> **God thus asserted: man is to believe**
> **Beyond what sense and reason can conceive,**
> **And for mysterious things of faith rely**
> **On the proponent, Heav'n's authority.**
> **If then our faith we for our guide admit,**
> **Vain is the farther search of human wit.**

Dryden's discouragement of reason as a means of discovering God is a way of introducing criticism of the Protestants at large who read the Scriptures over and over again trying to decide exactly what is meant. As in *Religio Laici*, Dryden is convinced that the Scripture is perfectly clear on the essential points; reason cannot adequately discover God, so why do the Protestants peruse the scriptures:

> **...why all this frantic pain**
> **To construe what his clearest words contain,**
> **And make a riddle what he made so plain?**
> **To take up half on trust, and half to try,**
> **Name it not faith, but bungling bigotry.**

Dryden is expressing the Catholic position that faith is the best means by which to bring about bliss; the Protestants, with their over-reliance on the Bible, cannot possibly bring themselves closer to God. Dryden turns to examine one particular group of Protestants, the Presbyterians, re-introduced as "th'insatiate Wolf." Dryden moves through a complex account of the history of the Presbyterians, mentioning Geneva, Zwingli, and Calvin. Dryden's present attitude as a Catholic had been well-summarized in lines 62-65 earlier:

What weight of ancient witness can prevail,
If private reason hold the public scale?
But, gracious God, how well dost thou provide
For erring judgments an unerring guide!

Dryden is now attacking the Presbyterians because they, unlike the Catholics, try to elevate imperfect, finite reason above faith.

Lines 212-307

Dryden continues his discussion of the Presbyterians, noting the way in which they thrive in England. He then enters into a digression concerning the creation of man: from his beginning, man has had a twin inheritance of reason and mercy, the one for ruling and the other for forgiving; reason was the law, while mercy was only a prerogative. Man, in his foolishness, misused his reason. Christ, "the blessed Pan," however, was merciful and so is King James II: "Such mercy from the British Lion shows." Dryden summarizes the terrible nuisance of the various Protestant or dissenter sects which he has represented as different animals, regretting that they should all have sprung up in England:

> O happy regions, Italy and Spain,
> Which never did those monsters entertain!
> The Wolf, the Bear, the Boar, can there advance
> No native claim of just inheritance.

None of these animals would dare attack the Hind; allegorically, the smaller splinter sects could not possibly threaten the established Roman Catholic Church. The Lion, King James II, is more powerful than the other animals and thus easily defends the Catholic Church; the other animals only "stand aloof, and tremble at his roar:/Much is their hunger, but their fear is more."

Lines 308-409

Dryden humorously refers to the fact that he has mentioned the major animals: "These are the chief; to number o'er the rest,/And stand, like Adam, naming ev'ry beast,/Were weary work..." Dryden then satirically announces that he will leave "These gross, half-animated lumps" that are incapable of thinking. He will now begin to discuss the Panther, representing the Church of England.

The opening description of the Panther is usually placed next to the equivalent introduction to the Hind in the opening lines of the poem. Dryden now writes:

> The Panther, sure the noblest, next the Hind,
> And fairest creature of the spotted king;
> O, could her inborn stains be wash'd away,

> She were too good to be a beast of prey.
> ....
> Her faults and virtues lie so mix'd that she
> Nor wholly stands condemn'd, nor wholly free.

The Hind, we recall, was "Without unspotted, innocent within," while the Panther is spotted on the outside and stained on the inside; the Church of England has none of the purity of the Catholic Church, and yet, Dryden insists, she has much more to recommend herself than do any of the other animals. There are virtues mixed in with her faults; it would be wrong either to praise or to condemn exclusively.

Dryden explains the rather unimpressive beginnings of the Church of England: King Henry VIII's love for Anne Boleyn led to the Reformation in England; Henry married her before officially receiving his divorce from Catherine of Aragon; thus Dryden says, "Then, by a left-hand marriage, weds the dame,/Cov'ring adult'ry with a specious name." He explains how, ever since, England has had difficulties. The Panther, the Church of England, endured, but in extreme discomfort; she followed the example of Luther who reinterpreted the Scriptures; the church pretended to have an established, ancient authority (like Catholicism), but in fact had none at all.

Lines 410-467

Dryden discusses the beliefs held by different religions with specific reference to the sacrament of the Eucharist. Catholics believe that the bread and wine are transformed into the body and blood of Christ; this is called transubstantiation. Other religions, such as the Lutheran, believe that Christ is actually present in the bread and wine. The Church of England believes instead that there is a "presence" -presumably spiritual - of Christ in the food and wine, but are vague with respect to the precise nature of the "presence." Thus Dryden says of the different beliefs: "one for substance, one for sign contends." He then reintroduces a familiar argument: one cannot have a religion based purely on the written word, because everyone will be able, ultimately, to interpret (and therefore act) as he pleases:

> As long as words a diff'rent sense will bear,
> And each may be his own interpreter,
> Our airy faith will no foundation find;
> The word's a weathercock for ev'ry wind:
> The Bear, the Fox, the Wolf, by turns prevail;
> The most in pow'r supplies the present gale.

Lines 468-571

Dryden continues his discussion of the problems of scriptural interpretation by mentioning how the Church of England, the Panther, attempts to gain further support from the Fathers and tradition because the Church and its councils are having difficulties; when troubles become great, she merely allows private conscience to be one's guide. But this concession, Dryden argues, not only removes authority from the Bible, but from the Church as well. If one can rely solely on one's conscience as a guide in all matters, it follows logically that one needs neither Church nor Scripture. Dryden says further, "Thus is the Panther neither lov'd nor fear'd,/A mere mock queen of a divided herd." Dryden feels that the Church of England is thus ruled as well as ruling. She submits some of her authority to the crowd by granting them freedom of interpretation.

The action of the allegory continues as Dryden describes the Panther as she wanders in melancholy one evening. The Hind is standing fearfully watching a watering place. When the Lion roars a warning that the Hind need not fear, she and her younglings go forward. At the same time, the other animals, including the Panther and the Wolf, watch her arrive. All of these observing animals are overpowered by the loveliness of the Hind:

> ...but nearer when they drew,
> And had the faultless object full in view,
> Lord, how they all admir'd her heav'nly hue!
> Some, who before her fellowship disdain'd,
> Scarce, and but scarce, from inborn rage restrain'd,
> Now frisk'd about her, and old kindred feign'd.
> Whether for love or int'rest, ev'ry sect
> Of all the savage nation shew'd respect.

This is Dryden's way of depicting the intensity and attraction of the purity of the Roman Catholic Church. This is also an example of the advantage in writing in the form of allegory; it seems credible enough for the other animals to be impressed by a beautiful hind, while it is impossible to conceive of a description of various sects bowing down and becoming friendly with the Catholic Church. When the other animals eventually begin to leave, the Panther approaches the Hind in order to start a discussion.

PART II: SUMMARY

Lines 572-708

Part II of *The Hind and the Panther* is a solid reflection of the title: it is an extended dialogue between the Hind and the Panther in which Dryden presents a variety of contemporary religious arguments. The Panther begins by telling the Hind that she has been lucky to escape trouble. The Hind replies that the Panther is also lucky; for, after all, many have argued that the Panther had been nursed in "Popery." The Church of England retained some of the forms and ceremonies of the Catholic Church while remaining silent ("dumb") regarding the main question - the meaning of the Eucharist. The Test Act has ended the necessity of remaining silent and the Panther has thus become newly loquacious. Now, says the Hind, the Panther is suddenly announcing that there is no presence of Christ in the bread and wine; for having abandoned this essential Catholic doctrine, the Church of England will not survive:

> And, to explain what your forefathers meant,
> By real presence in the sacrament,
> (After long fencing, push'd against a wall,)
> Your salvo comes, that he's not there at all:
> There chang'd your faith, and what may change may fall.

The Panther replies by saying that she never considered herself (unlike the Catholic Church) infallible. The Hind replies in a further discussion of the different interpretations of the Eucharist, accusing the Panther of changing its form frequently. The Panther smiles and answers by asking to know more of the source of "infallibility": "Is he from

Heav'n, this mighty champion, come,/Or lodg'd below in subterranean Rome?"

The Hind offers a long reply which is one of the more important statements in the poem as a whole. The Hind answers the Panther's request to know where "infallibility" resides by asserting that it is shared by the Pope and the Vatican Council; this is the moderate Catholic position of Dryden's time. (The more extreme position posited infallibility in the Pope alone.) The Hind first asserts that "The doubtful residence no proof can bring/Against the plain existence of the thing." Then the Hind says that the Pope and the Council share infallibility:

> I then affirm that this unfailing guide
> In Pope and gen'ral councils must reside;
> ....
> In Pope and council who denies the place,
> Assisted from above with God's unfailing grace?

The Hind then returns to one of Dryden's favorite (and, to a certain extent, overworked) subjects, the individualized Scriptural interpretations practiced widely by the various Protestant groups. Dryden writes:

> But mark how sandy is your own pretense,
> Who, setting councils, Pope, and Church aside,
> Are ev'ry man his own presuming guide.
> The sacred books, you say, are full and plain,
> And ev'ry needful point of truth contain:
> All, who can read, interpreters may be.
> No matter what dissension leaders make,
> Where ev'ry private man may save a stake:

> Rul'd by the Scripture and his own advice,
> Each has a blind by-path to Paradise.

Dryden's strong speech delivered by the Hind runs counter to the arguments he himself had made earlier in *Religio Laici*. We recall, for example, how he wrote that the Scriptures "Are uncorrupt, sufficient, clear, intire,/In all things which our needful faith require." Now, of course, those earlier views which he held are being expressed by the opposition, the Panther.

Lines 709-796

The Panther defends herself by saying that salvation is a possibility open to all people. She still insists that the Scriptures are clear: "The word in needful points is only plain," (1. 716). The Hind replies that she will not debate whether the points are needful or not; the fact remains that the theory of individual interpretation "Has led whole flocks, and leads them still astray/In weighty points, and full damnation's way." The Hind thinks that even all heretics can justify what they do or believe by citing the Bible: "Have not all heretics the same pretense/To plead the Scriptures in their own defense?" The Hind adds that the Panther has interfered with a tradition; when the Panther inquires in precisely what way, the Hind replies that the Panther mistakenly decided to base everything on the Scripture: "... all your faith you did on Scripture found." The Panther denies the charge, but the Hind declares that the Panther tries to rule the Scripture rather than be ruled by the Scripture. The Hind continues to attack the Panther's claim of the necessity of testing the tradition against the Scripture. This is not useful if the Panther, at the same time, is deciding what the Bible means:

> Thus, when you said tradition must be tried
> By Sacred Writ, whose sense yourselves decide,
> You said no more but that yourselves must be
> The judges of the Scripture sense, not we.

The Panther asks that if they do not appeal to the Scripture, how will they be able to distinguish between tradition which is pure and old, and that which is merely adulterated and new. The Hind promptly answers: by following the unbroken tradition of the Catholic Church which is transmitted from each generation to the next.

Lines 797-960

The Hind explains that the Panther has been ruined and led astray by the Wolf; that is, the Church of England has fallen under the bad influence of the Presbyterian Church. (The Presbyterians had frequently attacked the Catholics in the sermons of the time; theologically, they based everything on the Scripture.) The Church of England is a hybrid of the Presbyterians and Catholics; she is not committed in either direction and exists "like a mule made up of differing seed." The result is an endless series of new sects; and, Dryden points out, sects that are "extreme" loathe the "middle way." The Panther asks why Christ bothered to provide the Word, if tradition itself is sufficient. The Hind answers that Christ preached his faith before it was written down; the apostles were the first to receive the eternal truth directly and they established tradition. As the Hind states it:

> Our Savior preach'd his faith to humankind:
> From his apostles the first age receiv'd
> Eternal truth, and what they taught believ'd.

> **Thus by tradition faith was planted first;**
> **Succeeding flocks succeeding pastors nurs'd.**

The Hind further argues that Christ would have written his word down except that he foresaw the inevitable problems that would arise. Thus he instead spoke to the apostles and established an oral tradition: "Thus faith was ere the written word appear'd,/And men believ'd, not what they read, but heard." The Hind explains how the apostles wrote letters to be preached as sermons; in themselves they are not clear; they need the benefit of being taught, not simply written: "Clearness by frequent preaching must be wrought,/They writ but seldom, but they daily taught." The Hind's major argument is that the Scriptures are valuable only insofar as they are in the possession of the Church. Only the Catholic Church has an oral tradition evolved from the first teachers of Christ's Word; the truth of the apostles' learning can only be explicated by the Catholic Church because the apostles taught their immediate successors who in turn taught theirs; the "living guide," the spirit of the Catholic Church, is therefore an essential companion to the Bible.

Lines 961-1071

The Panther demands to know who "the living guide" is, and the Hind, in a dramatic point in the poem, looks up to the sky and pronounces, "She whom ye seek am I." The Hind renews her argument by asserting that the Church of England will not be able to dominate the various new sects. As long as she bases her authority only upon the Scripture, each sect can derive its own interpretation and challenge that offered by the Church of England. To assume that only she is correct (the Panther) is to reverse the Reformation. The church that is to dominate must have a unified basis of belief, but the Church of England does not have one because all of the various churches disagree. Every "reformed" church is inevitably isolated from every other reformed church; thus agreement is impossible. The only belief these different sects share is that they wish to be free from Catholic influence. Furthermore, if the various sects were to form a council (like the Vatican Council), no one sect would be allowed to preside; there could be no order. The logic of the Hind's argument is clear; there is far too much confusion among the various Protestant sects; they admit that someone guide is needed, but at the same time realize that they all err and thus "confess themselves are fallible." The only recourse is to turn to the natural church, the Catholic Church, that alone has infallibility:

> **Now since you grant some necessary guide,**
> **All who can err are justly laid aside**
>
> ....
>
> **It then remains, that Church can only be**
> **The guide, which owns unfailing certainty.**

Lines 1072-1219

Dryden presents, through the continuing speech of the Hind, an account of the coming of Christ and the origin of the Catholic Church. We hear of the "central principle of unity" which cements the Catholic Church together; this is the Church as described in the *Nicene Creed*, where one pledges belief in the Holy, Catholic, and Apostolic Church. The Hind charges the Panther with pretense at being Apostolic when, in effect, she may even have difficulty relating to the original Church (Catholic) of the Apostles. The Hind urges the supremacy of the Catholic Church and hopes that the Panther may perhaps be converted: "See how his Church, adorn'd with every grace,/With open arms, a king forgiving face,/Stands ready to prevent her long-lost son's embrace."

Lines 1220-1294

When the Hind has finished speaking, a bright stream of light flows from heaven; as the color of the sky signals approaching night, the Hind graciously invites the Panther to be her guest. The Panther hesitates, then accepts the offer and together they enter the Hind's cottage. The Hind points out that the Panther should consider becoming a permanent guest:

> So might these walls, with your fair presence blest,
> Become your dwelling place of everlasting rest,
> Not for a night, or quick revolving year;

That is, the Panther should consider converting. Part II concludes with a picture of the two of them lying down beside each other for an evening of sleep.

PART III: SUMMARY

Lines 1295-1424

Spenser's *Mother Hubbard's Tale*, a political beast **satire**, and *Aesop's Fables* are appealed to as precedents, just in case there are readers tempted to criticize Dryden's chosen form. As a general defense of the use of animals to represent various groups of men, Dryden writes: "If men transact like brutes, 't is equal then/For brutes to claim the privilege of men." Dryden then notes that the Hind need not fear spending the night with the Panther because the Lion would always protect her. (King James would always be careful that the Protestants not molest the Catholic Church; James of course had been very intolerant of the Protestants.) While the Panther and Hind are together, the scene is relatively peaceful. They have a meal together. After a while, the Hind and the Panther renew their debate and the Hind ends by saying that the Panther has no real reason to feel angry at the Catholic Church; rather it is the Wolf (the Presbyterians) who creates trouble.

Lines 1425-1572

The Panther replies that she does not hold grudges against the wealth of the Catholic Church. She then refers to her wish that her sons will not revolt; that is, that not too many sects claim independence from the Church of England. This comment causes the Hind to inquire precisely how many sons the Church of England has; many sects claim to be sons but in fact are not. As the Hind states:

> **Were you not dim, and doted, you might see**
> **A pack of cheats that claim a pedigree,**
> **No more of kin to you, than you to me.**

The Hind refers to one such group as "Your sons of latitude that court your grace," - a group of clergy and followers who departed from the English Church toward the end of the reign of Charles II and had been named the Latitudinarians. When the Hind says that they resulted from the Wolf's having been too busy in the Panther's bed, the implication is that they are the illegitimate offspring of the Panther and sired by the Wolf. The Catholic Church detested the Latitudinarians, and thus Dryden is severe. The Panther admits that some of her children are not particularly deserving, but adds, in defense, that at least the Sermon on the Mount was Protestant. The Hind agrees, as long as one holds the same view of the writings of Saint Peter and Saint Paul. The Hind continues her argument by saying that there are many who attempt to counterfeit the Catholic Church; as the Hind realizes she is becoming too outraged, she suddenly stops and pauses in meditation. Just as the lion rises eagerly to fight an equal opponent, she relaxes when the opponent is only cringing mildly on the ground.

Lines 1573-1703

The Hind resumes her speech and explains how she converts rebellious sons of her own. The Hind led Dryden to submit; now the Panther is urged to punish Stilling fleet for having reviled God's anointed king. The Panther is relieved that the Hind has not attacked any of her favorite sons. Then the Panther pursues the topic of conversion. The Panther speculates on the happiness of those who have converted, but then concludes by saying, "Methinks in those who firm with me remain,/It shows a nobler principle than gain." The Hind replies that the Panther would be right if hers were the suffering side; but, in fact, it is not. The Hind attacks proselytes who convert without sound reasons.

Lines 1704-1932

We now arrive at one of the most important and carefully constructed sections of *The Hind and the Panther*. The

Panther offers a fable of the swallows in order to discuss the situation of the English Catholics. In summary: the swallows, who symbolize the English Catholics, were ruined because they followed the wrong advice of the Martins, the extremists who persuaded the Catholics not to leave England.

The Panther opens the story by explaining how the swallows, who, as representative of the English Catholics, were "privileg'd above the rest/Of all the birds." The swallows migrate at different times of the year: They come to council and agree on a tentative day to depart. The young birds are shivering and frightened and request that their parents wait and fly on another day. At this point the Martin, "A Church-begot, and church-believing bird;/Of little body, but of lofty mind," persuades the swallows not to leave. It has been suggested that the Martin represents Petre, the king's counselor in both political and spiritual matters, who persuaded the Catholics not to leave England; as Dryden summarizes the Martin's position: "...so his advice/Was present safety, bought at any price." Some of the swallows are not anxious to heed the advice of the Martin and feel that "their only danger was delay." The swallows decide to vote and "'t was carried by the major part to stay." Once the swallows agree not to leave, the Martin acquires a new power; at the same time, he does not ask that they pray too much: "For Martin much devotion did not ask;/They pray'd sometimes, and that was all their task."

Finally a "Cuckow" sings. As his song usually proclaims the coming of spring, the swallows prepare to leave: "No longer doubting, all prepare to fly." The swallows begin to fly and breed; eventually their number increases enough for them to leave for new lands. Many of the birds fly up into the air, but suddenly there is an eclipse. That morning the sun had entered Capricorn, thus eclipsing the moon; the picture of the birds clashing into each other in total darkness is vividly presented:

> **The crowd, amaz'd, pursued no certain mark;**
> **But birds met birds, and justled in the dark:**
> **Few mind the public in a panic fright;**
> **And fear increas'd the horror of the night.**
> **Night came, but unattended with repose;**
> **Alone she came, no sleep their eyes to close.**

The picture symbolizes the state of confusion into which the English Catholics are thrown when an evil or unforeseen event - such as the death of James - suddenly occurs. The Martin himself is captured and tried for treason, because the laws (line 1927) made by Queen Elizabeth and confirmed by James I provided that any Catholic priest caught on English soil would be liable to the charge of high treason.

The Panther's fable of the swallows has thus insultingly depicted the English Catholics. Naturally then, the Hind is provoked.

Lines 1933-2049

The Hind refers to the "malice" of the Panther's fable. She also suggests more positively that the Martin had represented Martin Luther. Although of course unhappy that there should have been such a son in the Catholic Church, the Hind assures the panther that such sons are also lurking in the Anglican Church. The Hind then wishes that the differences between the two churches could be settled:

> What angry pow'r prevents our present peace?
> The Lion, studious of our common good,
> Desires (and kings' desires are ill withstood)
> To join our nations in a lasting love;
> The bars betwixt are easy to remove,
> For sanguinary laws were never made above.

The Hind then laments bitterly the extent of Catholic persecution in England, specifically that conveyed through the Test Act; the Hind feels that the Act not only prevents Catholics from obtaining positions of importance but further allows weak people to obtain them:

> But that unfaithful Test unfound will pass
> The dross of atheists, and sectarian brass:
> As if th'experiment were made to hold
> For base productions, and reject the gold.

The Hind argues that although England professes tolerance, she does not practice it.

Lines 2050-2195

The Panther argues that the Hind arrives in England like Aeneas arriving in Italy - claiming that by long possession the land is his. The Panther says that he acts on conscience. The Hind argues that "conscience" is a weak excuse, more often meaning "interest." By way of conscience, one can justify almost any action: "O Proteus Conscience, never to be tied." The Panther defends herself by insisting that England simply cannot allow Catholic infiltration; once allowed entrance, Catholics would strive for domination. The Panther refers specifically to the way in which Catholicism lurks menacingly outside the shore of England:

> These are my banks your ocean to withstand,
> Which proudly rising overlooks the land;
> And, once let in, with unresisted sway,
> Would sweep the pastors and their flocks away.

The Panther then wishes that the Catholic Church would wait for a "more auspicious planet" to colonize. The Hind objects to this scornful remark. She says England need not fear the water usurping her banks if England is in fact in the right; her fear and her reliance on unfair laws (like the Test Act) suggest she knows she is wrong:

> Your care about your bank infers a fear
> Of threat'ning floods and inundations near;
> ....
> T'intrench in what you grant unrighteous laws,
> Is to distrust the justice of your cause,
> And argues that the true religion lies
> In those weak adversaries you despise.

The Hind then goes on to discuss the theory that kings derive their power from the people, a view previously discussed by Dryden in *Absalom and Achitophel*. The Panther continues to argue and then asks "what concord there could be/Betwixt two kinds whose natures disagree."

Lines 2196-2360

We now arrive at a second beast fable, one which again represents one of the most interesting and important parts of the poem. Dryden decides that the Hind will tell "a wholesome tale" in "homely style." The Hind first begins by saying there once was "a plain good man," introducing, symbolically, King James II. This man enjoyed success and shared it by being generous to the Doves who live near his hall. Allegorically, the Doves represent the clergy of the Church of England. Dryden's depiction of them is harshly satiric:

> **A sort of Doves were hous'd too near their hall,**
> **Who cross the proverb, and abound with gall.**
> **Tho' some, 't is true, are passively inclin'd,**
> **The greater part degenerate from their kind;**
> **Voracious birds, that hotly bill and breed,**
> **And largely drink, because on salt they feed.**
> **..**
> **The more they fed, they raven'd still for more.**

As a sharp contrast to this depiction of the English clergy, Dryden presents a picture of the few Catholic clergy that James II also maintained:

> **Another farm he had behind his house,**
> **Not over stock'd, but barely for his use;**
> **Wherein his poor domestic poultry fed,**
> **And from his pious hands receiv'd their bread.**

Dryden continues to develop a contrast between the doves (sometimes called Pigeons) and the poor poultry. The Catholic clergy are also symbolized by the cock. There are numerous references to the nuns (sister Partlet); to the way in which priests get up in the middle of the night to pray; and then to the English clergy as "birds of Venus," suggesting that unlike the Catholic priests, they do not subscribe to celibacy. As for the people, they of course prefer the Doves: "But sure the common cry was all for these,/Whose life and precept both encourag'd ease." Furthermore, the Doves spend a great deal of their time trying to make the poultry seem dangerous and undesirable.

Lines 2361-2514

The Hind refers again to a law which has forbidden the poultry to walk on the farms (i.e., the Test Act). She explains further:

> **Their foes a deadly shibboleth devise:**
> **By which unrighteously it was decreed**
> **That none to trust, or profit, should succeed,**
> **Who would not swallow first a poisonous wicked weed.**

This refers to the Test Act's requirement that one swear disbelief in the Catholic doctrine of transubstantiation. Although the man (the king) tried to repeal the law, the doves insisted that it be maintained and "New doubts indeed they daily strove to raise." Because the poultry are thus depicted as a threat, the doves decide that they should requisition some potent bird of prey to attack the poultry. They decide on the Buzzard, a name generally connoting ignorance in Dryden's day, who allegorically represents Gilbert Burnet. In the course of a long career as an historian, politician, and polemicist, Burnet had championed the Church of England. *The Buzzard* (This whole section of the poem, incidentally, is sometimes referred to as the fable of the Buzzard) is quick to accept the Doves' invitation to come and ravage the Catholic cocks. Dryden pictures the Buzzard in harsh, invective terms; the **satire** is perfect in such comments as "all his hate on trivial points depends" and "his praise of foes is venomously nice." Dryden describes him, satirically, as being "satire-proof":

> Prompt to assail, and careless of defense,
> Invulnerable in his impudence,
> He dares the world; and, eager of a name,
> He thrusts about, and justles into fame.
> Frontless and satire-proof, he scours the streets,
> And runs an Indian muck at all he meets.

The Buzzard and his following of Doves dig their bills into the chickens maliciously as the poem continues.

Lines 2515-2592

The Hind continues her tale by explaining that when the "imperial owner," King James, observed the way in which the Doves, with the help of the Buzzard, were turning his grace into villainy, he "pronounc'd a doom/Of sacred strength for ev'ry age to come." That is, he passed the Declaration of Indulgence, allowing both Catholics and dissenters the freedom to worship as they pleased:

> He therefore makes all birds of ev'ry sect
> Free of his farm, with promise to respect
> Their sev'ral kinds alike, and equally protect.
> His gracious edict the same franchise yields
> To all the wild encrease of woods and fields.

The Buzzard and his followers depart and the Hind ends her tale. The Panther affects a yawn, light begins to appear from the rising sun, and the Hind and the Panther part company.

Comment And Analysis: It is worth noting that *The Hind and the Panther* ends inconclusively. Neither the Hind nor the Panther can be said to have emerged the winner.

The poem is not presented as a contest which must have a winner and a loser, but rather as an intellectual dialogue. The Hind and the Panther argue, become angry, make friends, become angry again, and then are quiet; there is a simple vacillation between a poetry of debate and that of allegory. The poem is designed as a vehicle for carrying the statement of Dryden's reasons for converting to Catholicism. The satire is not sharp or invective until Part III, where there is a depiction of the gluttonous Doves as symbolic of the English clergy. The mere fact that the Hind and the Panther can settle down together for the night suggests that Dryden would be happy to see a reconciliation between the Catholic Church and the Church of England. As he points out (in line 1960, ff.), the king is anxious to establish peace between the two churches. And the king of course does resolve the conflict between the doves and the chickens by passing the Declaration of Indulgence which, we recall, was issued just prior to Dryden's publication of the poem.

One of the major problems associated with Dryden's *The Hind and The Panther* is its length. We move from Dryden's personal statement in favor of Catholicism in Part I, through the lengthy dialogue between the Hind and the Panther in Part II, and then, finally, through the even lengthier Part III, with its blend of continued dialogue and beast fable. Each part is longer than the preceding one. Parts of the poem are generally considered very good - the original presentation of the Hind, the Panther, and the various other animals, most noticeably the Wolf; the statements on the limits of human reason (also dramatically rendered in *Religio*

Laici); the two fables, that of the swallows told by the Panther, and that of the Buzzard told by the Hind. But these parts are still only parts. The fact remains that a great deal of the poem - particularly the long, specialized theological debates in Part II - is downright boring; it was tediously written and thus is only tediously read. The poem's organization is not of the same high quality as the poem's more brilliant passages.

Form And Style: It is impossible to know whether Dryden thought his *The Hind and the Panther* would revive an interest in the poetic community in the literary genre of the beast fable. Previously popular in the works of such writers as Aesop, Chaucer, and Spenser, the beast fable was not a particularly popular genre in Dryden's time. In any case, no "revival" occurred.

Probably the most appealing use of animal allegory in the poem is discovered in the two final fables. The contrast developed between the doves and the chickens is one of the best features of the poem, both from the point of view of interest and from that of technique. The larger allegory, that revolving solely around the Hind and the Panther, is somehow less desirable. The overall structure of the poem, based on the continued dialogue between these two animal characters, is weakened through the digressions; and yet, ironically, without the digressions, the poem would be of relatively limited substance. The conclusion one must draw is that the mere contrast inherent in the juxtaposed images of the Hind and the Panther is simply not that dramatic.

ESSAY QUESTIONS AND ANSWERS

Question: To what extent is *The Hind and the Panther* a biographical poem?

Answer: The major importance of *The Hind and the Panther* is not its biographical comment on the reasons behind Dryden's conversion in particular. Rather, it is important because it demonstrates -sometimes vividly - the primary theological arguments of Dryden's day. In *Religio Laici*, Dryden was writing as a member of the Church of England; now he is writing as a Catholic. Yet in both poems we are exposed to the respective positions of Anglicans and Catholics. Dryden now may be first a Catholic, but nevertheless he still sincerely longs for peace between the two churches. Dryden's depiction of the English clergy is so much more severe and malicious than his depiction of the Panther herself that it is probable that he wrote this last section after the king had become more annoyed at the Anglican Church. *The Hind and the Panther* is colored everywhere with Dryden's personal feelings, but those that were commonly held still dominate; the original presentation of the allegorical animals is largely modeled upon the prevailing opinions of the English public. Biography, in short, has a part in the poem, but should not be seen as the poem's dominant element.

Question: With regard to the theological debate in *The Hind and the Panther*, what is the main recurrent theme?

Answer: Dryden's insistence on the weakness of individualized scriptural interpretation. Throughout the poem, but particularly in Part II, Dryden attributes the fundamental weakness of the Protestant (dissenting) religions as that of excessive freedom of interpretation. By allowing each individual to interpret the scriptures as he pleases, the scriptures loose their validity as a final authority. Nothing can be certain if explained differently by different readers. We recall that Father Simon had attacked the Bible itself in order to persuade people that they had no sure recourse except in the authority of the Catholic Church. Dryden of course answered this attack in his *Religio Laici*. Now, to achieve the same result sought by Father Simon - increased attention to the Catholic Church - Dryden attacks not the Bible itself but the Protestants' doctrine of individual interpretation. Again and again Dryden crystallizes this freedom as the central error in the Protestant way of thought. Furthermore, such freedom means that the various sects will never be able to have good relationships with one another; because each sect is free to interpret the Scripture as it pleases, it will have no need of the Anglican church:

> **Your only rule of faith the Scriptures are,**
> **Interpreted by men of judgment sound,**
> **Which ev'ry sect will for themselves expound;**
> **Nor think less re'rence to their doctors due**
> **For sound interpretation, than to you. (lines 997-1001)**

ODES

In addition to his **satires** and long verse letters, Dryden wrote many short lyrical poems. His comedies and Miscellanies contain a large number of light, sparkling songs written in the "Cavalier" tradition of love. But even more important are his "odes." In his time, an "ode" designated a Cowleyan Pindaric ode - which was, in short, a rhymed poem of various irregular verses arranged in **stanzas** of different length with no fixed structure. With the exception of the requirement that there be **rhyme**, the ode form was essentially formless. Dryden wrote five such odes: the Threnodia Augustalis (1685) which celebrated the deceased King Charles II; To The Pious Memory of Mrs. Anne Killigrew which celebrated the prematurely stricken poetess of that name; and three odes set to music, On the Death of Mr. Henry Purcell (Henry Purcell was one of the great musical composers of the day), Song for St. Cecilia's Day, and Alexander's Feast. We will here consider briefly the three odes generally acknowledged to be the most interesting and the more important of the five.

TO ANNE KILLIGREW

Introduction

The full title reads: "To The Pious Memory of the Accomplis'd Young Lady, Mrs. Anne Killigrew, excellent in the two sister-arts of poesy and painting, an ode." Anne Killigrew, the daughter of a clergyman and minor dramatist, Henry Killigrew, was born in the year of the Restoration, 1660, and then died tragically of smallpox in 1685. During this year, an edition of her Poems appeared. Samuel Johnson called Dryden's poem "the noblest ode that our language has ever produced," and E. M. W. Tillyard has referred to it as a "masterpiece."

SUMMARY

Stanzas 1-3

Dryden begins by addressing the deceased young Mrs. (mistress - a label applied to both married and unmarried women) Killigrew as the "youngest virgin-daughter of the skies,/Made in the last promotion of the blest." He wonders precisely which part of heaven she inhabits. That the poem is not solely about a particular person but rather about a person who symbolizes all great poetesses becomes clear when Dryden begins to speculate how she became so lovely a poetess. She might, by "traduction," have been influenced by her father's poetry; she might, on the other hand, be the reincarnation of the Greek poetess Sappho. But in any case, when she was born, both heaven and earth sang, rejoicing in her beauty; people even heard the music of the spheres:

> Thy brother-angels at thy birth
> Strung each his lyre, and tun'd it high,
> That all the people of the sky
> Might know a poetess was born on earth.
> And then, if ever, mortal ears
> Had heard the music of the spheres!

Stanzas 4-7

Dryden departs from a description of the joy at Anne Killigrew's birth to a depiction of the low state into which contemporary poetry has fallen. Dryden is sad and ashamed when he surveys the low, bawdy, obscene literature of the Restoration; he is presenting his opinion as a planned, direct contrast to the preceding **stanzas** describing loveliness:

> O gracious God! how far have we
> Profan'd thy heav'nly gift of poesy!
> Made prostitute and profligate the Muse,
> Debas'd to each obscene and impious use,
> Whose harmony was first ordain'd above
> For tongues of angels, and for hymns of love!

Dryden considers this recent decline of poetry the second "fall" of man and asks if Mrs. Killigrew's death can atone for it. In **stanza** five he enlarges on the beauty and natural grace of Anne Killigrew's poetry, and then in **stanzas** six and seven explains how she was not content to master only one kind of art - poetry - but turned to a second - painting - in which she also excelled, particularly in her rendering of people and of pastoral settings. Sometimes her paintings were even more lovely than she had imagined they could be.

Stanzas 8-10

Dryden describes the way in which Anne Killigrew slowly died of smallpox. He also refers to "Orinda," that is Mrs. Phillips, a young poetess whom Anne Killigrew admired and to whom she dedicated some verses, who had also died of smallpox. Then Dryden informs Anne Killigrew's brother, Henry, a naval officer, that he shall never embrace his sister again; if, however, he sees a new-kindled star among the Pleiades, he will know it is she. The ode concludes with Dryden assuring all that Anne Killigrew will be among the first to show the way to heaven when Judgment Day arrives.

Comment And Analysis: Dryden's ode to Mrs. Killigrew contains some very beautiful poetry; the subject matter is both lovely and grim. The opening address to the poetess, the references to her poetry and painting, and the ode's final lines all capture the natural beauty and talent enjoyed by Anne Killigrew. But we also have some somber notes - the description of the way in which the smallpox slowly ruined her lovely body, and the references to the way in which the bodies of poets will leave their burial places first because covered with the least dirt. The beauty and ugliness are not incompatible; the latter only sharpens the essence of the former and thus together work effectively to illuminate the memory of Anne Killigrew.

Several major things are happening in the poem. First we learn of the circumstances of the poetess' birth, then of her productivity in the two arts of poetry and painting, and then of her death by smallpox; the order

is thus chronological, but throughout the poem we are aware of her as a divine spirit, one already enjoying the next life. The digression on the baseness of the contemporary Restoration literature (stanza 4) is more of a side excursion than an integral part of the poem. The greater contrast is between Mrs. Killigrew's joy - filled life and her tragic way of dying (but not her death itself, which has inherent beauty).

Form And Style: Dryden's poem fulfills the requirements of the formal, conventional, popular Pindaric Ode: each stanza is of different length and overall structure, while each is still composed in rhyming poetry. The language of this ode is of far greater evocative power than Dryden's longer poems, and many consider the ideas more poetically expressed than those in the two St. Cecilia's Day odes.

A SONG FOR ST. CECILIA'S DAY

Introduction

A London musical society had started the custom of celebrating November 22, the feast of St. Cecelia (the patroness of music) five years before it asked Dryden to contribute the following ode in 1687. The subject of this ode, naturally associated with a celebration of music, is an explanation of the classical idea that the universe achieves an overall harmony through the existence of opposing, clashing elements.

SUMMARY

The ode opens with a careful explanation of the central idea in the background of the poem that the world was created in harmony: "From harmony, from heav'nly harmony/This universal frame began." But the harmony is achieved out of warring elements - "a heap/of jarring atoms." Dryden explains the power of music to stir the passions and then evocatively describes several musical instruments: the trumpet, with its loud clangor, can excite us to arms; the soft notes of the flute capture the "woes of hopeless lovers"; sharp violins can well proclaim "Their jealous pangs, and desperation,/Fury, frantic indignation." But no instrument can equal the abilities and the beauty of the organ whose notes inspire "holy love": in particular, vocal breath was given to Cecilia's organ; when an angel heard the sound, she mistakenly began to come to earth, thinking that she was traveling toward heaven. In the final chorus we are told that when the last trumpet blows, ending the existence of the universe, the music of the spheres will also cease and the sky will be "untuned":

> **So, when the last and dreadful hour**
> **This crumbling pageant shall devour,**
> **The trumpet shall be heard on high,**
> **The dead shall live, the living die,**
> **And Music shall untune the sky.**

Comment And Analysis: The essence of music has been captured in Dryden's ode. It was, appropriately, set to music, first by the Italian composer Draghi, and eventually in the eighteenth century by Handel. The ode was first published as a "broadside" (a single sheet of paper with only the ode printed on it) in 1687 and then appeared in his 1693 Examen Poeticum. One of Dryden's major early critics, Joseph Warton, had this to say about the "Ode on St. Cecilia's Day":

If Dryden had never written anything but this Ode, his name would have been immortal... It is difficult to find new terms to express our admiration of the variety, richness, and melody of its numbers; the force, beauty, and distinctness of its images; the succession of so many different passions and feelings; and the matchless perspicuity of its diction. The scene opens, in the first stanza, in an awful and august matter... No particle of it can be wished away, but the epigrammatic turn of the four concluding lines.

Warton's harsh judgment of the last lines of the ode has not been endorsed by very many critics; but it is acknowledged that the ode is one of Dryden's most splendid creations. Although Dryden was writing the musical ode as a poetic convention of his time, he nevertheless achieved new things. Dr. Johnson thought this ode was "lost in the splendor of the second" (i.e., "Alexander's Feast"), but that had it been writen by any other poet, it would have recommended him.

Form And Style: It is appropriate when writing a musical ode to strive for musical effects in the words and versification. This Dryden does admirably, particularly in the central section of the poem, as he moves from one instrument to another with corresponding changes in versification. The bold pronouncement of the trumpets captures the sound of these instruments: "The trumpet's loud clangor/Excites us to arms." And so is the music of the flute crystallized in the words: "The soft complaining Flute/In dying notes discovers/The woes of hopeless lovers." But as John Hollander has suggested (in his book, *The Untuning Of The Sky*, titled after a line from this ode), the first and last sections of the ode are the most distinguished, for in both, Dryden seems to present a major statement about music. Some critics, like Johnson, have objected to the antithetical coupling of "music" and "untuning" in the last lines, but it is generally agreed that this is appropriate in view of the overall form of the ode, and as a stylistic reference back to the opening statement about the universe's having been created in harmony.

ALEXANDER'S FEAST

Introduction

Ten years after writing the "Ode to St. Cecilia," Dryden wrote a second ode celebrating this saint, entitled: "Alexander's Feast, or The Power of Music; an Ode in Honor of St. Cecilia's Day." It was again written for a London musical society. This second of the Cecilia Odes, generally considered Dryden's best, was first set to music by Jerimiah Clarke, and eventually by Handel, in 1736. Dryden knew very well that it may have been the best thing he had written; as he wrote in a letter to Tonson near the end of 1697: "I am glad to hear from all hands, that my Ode is esteem'd the best of all my poetry, by all the town: I thought so my self when I writ it; but being old, I mistrusted my own judgment. I hope it has done you service, and will do more." Sir Walter Scott selected "Alexander's Feast" as Dryden's best lyric.

SUMMARY

Dryden takes as his subject the way in which Alexander the Great, who was the son of Philip of Macedon and the lover of Thais, was influenced by the musician Timotheus to set fire to the Persian city of Persepolis where he was enjoying a victory feast. The poem opens with the setting of the royal feast in celebration of the winning of Persia; Alexander sits exultant on a throne with the lovely Thais by his side. We are introduced to the musician Timotheus with his lyre, and then told that Alexander was born the son of Jove and Olympia; thus the "sov'reign of the world" created the conqueror of the world. The god of wine, Bacchus, is presented and the scene is filled with drunken revelry and lethargy. The music becomes intensified and Alexander is prompted to make love to Thais. The idea is reiterated in the chorus (**stanza** 5):

> **The prince, unable to conceal his pain,**
>   **Gaz'd on the fair**
>   **Who caus'd his care,**
>   **And sigh'd and look'd, sigh'd and look'd,**
> **Sigh'd and look'd, and sigh'd again:**
> **At length, with love and wine at once oppress'd,**
> **The vanquish'd victor sunk upon her breast.**

This explanation of Alexander resting on Thais achieves lethargic splendor through the careful repetition of the sighing.

We have a sharp, sudden transition away from this lethargy as Timotheus begins to strike his lyre harder and harder, crying for revenge. Alexander, again inspired by Timotheus, picks up a torch ("flambeau") and, following

Thais, sets the city on fire (as Helen had once set fire to Troy). In the last **stanza**, Dryden summarizes the way in which the playing of Timotheus could inspire madness:

> **Thus, long ago,**
> **Ere heaving bellows learn'd to blow,**
> **While organs yet were mute;**
> **Timotheus, to his breathing flute,**
> **And sounding lyre,**
> **Could swell the soul to rage, or kindle soft desire.**

While the organs yet were mute, as the poem ends, we see Cecilia arriving with her "vocal frame" (that is the organ) which again - as in the earlier "Ode to St. Cecilia" - is the most exquisite instrument. Timotheus, with his lyre, can raise a mortal (Alexander) to the skies, but Cecilia, as a more impressive act, can bring an angel down to earth while it thinks itself traveling to heaven; this hyperbole, used already in the earlier Cecilia ode, is repeated in the final chorus:

> **At last, divine Cecilia came,**
> **Inventress of the vocal frame;**
> **The sweet enthusiast, from her sacred store,**
> **Enlarg'd the former narrow bounds,**
> **And added length to solemn sounds,**
> **With nature's mother wit, and arts unknown before.**
> **Let old Timotheus yield the prize,**
> **Or both divide the crown;**
> **He rais'd a mortal to the skies;**
> **She drew an angel down.**

Comment And Analysis: Not that much happens in "Alexander's Feast." In review, Alexander is inspired by

Timotheus' music to burn down a city; but even that powerful music is nothing when compared to the music of Cecilia with her organ; the whole point of the poem is well summarized in the closing couplet - "He rais'd a mortal to the skies;/She drew an angel down." The entire ode is, in short, one extended hyperbole. We read the poem as a stylistic exercise. In Dryden's day, poems in praise of music for St. Cecilia's Day celebrations were very common. As in Cowley's Pindaric Odes, we find in Dryden's Ode an extravagance, an exhibitionist series of metrical changes and sound effects. One has to quote the entire ode in order to demonstrate the versatility and surprises it contains. As David Daiches has accurately suggested, Dryden's Ode is "fine verbal fireworks."

Form And Style: The style of Dryden's most popular ode, "Alexander's Feast," is primarily baroque - that is, fancy, exhibitionist, ornate. There is an excessive stylistic richness which we find in other Pindaric odes, all written so deliberately in strange patterns. The changes made when moving from stanza to stanza, the repetition of the chorus, the echoes, the musical cadence, and the weird modulations all combine to prove that the ode is a form designed for the poet intending to be a poet primarily in the sense of technical craftsmanship.

QUESTIONS AND ANSWERS ON THE ODES

Question: Is there an improvement in Dryden's style when moving from the first to the second of his St. Cecilia's Day odes?

Answer: No, it is difficult to prove that the second ode is better than the one written ten years earlier. The first is shorter, and has much shorter **stanzas** and, further, does not have the choruses which Dryden includes in the second. The second Ode has a more ornate quality of expression; there are more complicated, fancy transitions; there are more intensified **rhymes** and repetitive chants, such as "None but the brave" in the first **stanza**. And yet the second ode does not seem to say as much to us as the compact, more unifed first ode. In the second, the fact that Dryden does not have a great deal to say is suggested by his reiteration in the ending of the same point made in the first ode. In the "Ode to St. Cecilia" we have some beautiful poetry coupled with statements of universal significance with regard to the lasting beauty and power of music. In "Alexander's Feast" we have only one instance of music's power - as Alexander is urged to burn down a city. To give this second ode a universal significance, Dryden must return to his treatment of Cecilia with her organ in the earlier ode. Thus although the second ode may be more stylistically decorated and lavish, it seems to lack the meaning and beauty of the shorter, earlier ode.

Question: How does the digression on Restoration literature relate to the rest of the ode on Anne Killigrew?

Answer: Dryden's harsh comments on the low quality of contemporary literature should be viewed - from the point of view of the organization of the ode - primarily as a digression. This is not to say that this digression (**stanza** four) does not belong in the ode. Indeed, it does. Stanza three is referring to the divinity behind poetry. **Stanza** four follows logically as a contrast:

> **O gracious God! how far have we**
> **Profan'd thy heav'nly gift of poesy!**

Two things are happening in **stanza** four: on the one hand, Dryden is asserting that the proper essence of poetry is divine and beautiful; on the other hand he is asserting that the improper essence of poetry is worldly and obscene. As the proper kind Is demonstrated in the poetry of the dead poetess Anne Killigrew, so the improper kind is demonstrate in the poetry of Restoration drama. In other words, the digression does indeed provide a contrast enhancing Anne Killigrew's memory; but, at the same time, a larger contrast is being made, one that is more central to the meaning of the poem - that between the music of the spheres and the silence of the spheres which will result when the last trumpet sounds. Now this is the exact conclusion in "an Ode For St. Cecilia's Day," while only a suggested conclusion in the ode to Anne Killigrew. But in any case, the important contrast between life and death is developed by means other than the contrast implied in the digression into Restoration literature. Whether this ode was the appropriate place for Dryden's comments on contemporary literature or not is another question; suffice it to say that the digression is not illogically included in the poem, but neither is it central to the poem's meaning.

CRITICAL COMMENTARY

From the very day Dryden died, poets and critics alike have had something to say about him. Like any poet, Dryden's reputation has sometimes faltered and sometimes been enhanced. Sir John Shadwell, the son of the Shadwell whom we recall Dryden attacked so vigorously, wrote from Paris when Dryden died, "the men of letters here lament the loss of Mr. Dryden very much. The honors paid to him have done our countrymen no small service." The English press was, expectedly, suffused with poems of praise for the deceased Dryden; even his old enemies contributed. Dryden was buried in the Poet's Corner in Westminster Abbey, while Europe sensed the passing of an extremely versatile poet.

A minor Restoration playwright, George Farquhar, had a less admirable but nevertheless partially accurate way of interpreting Dryden's baroque funeral, seeing in the funeral the same irregularity which persisted in Dryden's various experiments at writing different kinds of poetry: "he was an extraordinary man, and buried after an extraordinary fashion, for I do believe there was never such another burial seen... And so much for Mr. Dryden; whose burial was the same as his life, variety, and not of a piece: the quality and mob, farce and heroics: the sublime and ridiculous mixed in a piece; great Cleopatra in a hackney coach." It would of course be both naive and unfair to take Farquhar's comment as an accurate summary of Dryden's life as a poet! But many things have been said about Dryden and his poetry; a brief survey of the more important statements follows.

WILLIAM CONGREVE ON DRYDEN

William Congreve, the master of the "comedy of manners" and friend to men like Swift, Steele, and Pope, had been admired and respected by Dryden for many years; and furthermore, Congreve had valued Dryden's friendship highly. After Dryden died, Congreve did not write any more plays. In 1717 Congreve issued a complete edition of Dryden's plays; he wrote of Dryden: "He was of a nature exceedingly humane and compassionate… His friendship, where he professed it, went beyond his professions. He was of very easy, very pleasing access; but somewhat slow, and, as it were, diffident in his advance to others… As his reading had been very extensive, so was he very happy in a memory tenacious of everything he had read… He was extremely ready and gentle in his correction of the errors of any writer who thought fit to consult him, and full as ready and patient to admit the reprehension of others, in respect of his own oversights or mistakes."

SAMUEL JOHNSON ON DRYDEN

In the first paragraph of his famous "Life of John Dryden," Johnson begins by quoting the above passage (more fully) by Congreve, noting it is the only statement we have about Dryden the man. Johnson's ensuing discussion of the various aspects of Dryden's writing is fascinating and probably the best place for the student to begin his investigation into Dryden. Perhaps Johnson's most important (and best known) statement is in citing Dryden as "the father of English criticism," but for our purposes we are primarily interested in surveying Johnson's opinions of Dryden the poet, for Johnson also recognized that "the criticism of Dryden is the criticism of a poet." Johnson credited Dryden with reforming English poetic **diction**: "There was therefore, before the time of Dryden, no poetical **diction**, no system of words at once refined from the grossness of domestic use, and free from the harshness of terms appropriated to particular arts...the new versification, as it was called, may be considered as owing its establishment to Dryden; from whose time it is apparent that English poetry has had no tendency to relapse to its former savageness."

JOHNSON ON THE POEMS

Johnson's discussion of those particular poems which we have examined is rigorous and interesting. Johnson considered *Annus Mirabilis* one of Dryden's "greatest attempts." The poem was "written with great diligence, yet does not fully answer the expectation raised by such subjects and such a writer." In other words, Johnson approved more of the subject than the precise way in which Dryden developed it. In his typical way of pointing out both good and bad (which was why Lord Macaulay objected to some of Johnson's critiques), Johnson writes of *Absalom and Achitophel*: "(it) is a work so well known that particular criticism is superfluous. If it be considered as a poem political and controversial, it will be found to comprise all the excellences of which the subject is susceptible - acrimony of censure, variety and vigor of sentiment, happy turns of language, and pleasing harmony of numbers - and all these raised to such a height as can scarcely be found in any other English composition. It is not, however, without faults; some lines are inelegant or improper, and too many are irreligiously licentious. The original structure of the poem was defective; allegories drawn to great length will always break; Charles could not run continually parallel with David." It is obvious that Johnson objected to *Absalom and Achitophel* partially on the grounds that all allegories are weak. As for *The Medal*, Johnson considered it written upon the same principles as *Absalom and Achitophel*: not as interesting, but just as well written.

ON "RELIGIO" AND "THE HIND"

Johnson hoped to find a more personal statement by Dryden in the *Religio Laici*; when he did not find such a statement, he complained: "*Religio Laici*...is almost the only work of Dryden which can be considered as a voluntary effusion; in this, therefore, it might be hoped that the full effulgence of his genius would be found. But unhappily the subject is rather argumentative than poetical: he intended only a specimen of metrical disputation." Even more annoying, to Johnson's mind, was the way in which Dryden mixed personal with impersonal, and light with serious in *Religio Laici*; although prosaic in some parts, and mixed in attitude, Johnson nevertheless admitted that *Religio Laici* was probably the best of this kind of poem. Johnson was less impressed by the similar poem, *The Hind and the Panther*. Although it is the longest of Dryden's original works and a logical allegory, Johnson still thought that "the scheme of the work is injudicious and incommodious; for what can be more absurd than that one beast should counsel another to rest her faith upon a pope and council... The Hind at one time is afraid to drink at the common brook, because she may be worried; but walking home with the Panther talks by the way of the Nicene Fathers, and at last declares herself to be the Catholic Church." This absurdity was very properly ridiculed in the *Country Mouse and the City Mouse of Montague and Prior*.

ON THE LATER ODES

Johnson lavished the most praise on Dryden's later odes. He called Dryden's ode to Anne Killigrew "the noblest ode that our language ever has produced:" The first part of the ode flowed, in Johnson's view, "with a torrent of enthusiasm." He considered Dryden's first Ode for Cecilia's Day "lost in the splendor of the second," but admitted that it contained passages "which would have dignified any other poet." Later in his critique, Johnson returns to these two odes, stating what must have been his most considered opinion: "One composition must however be distinguished. The Ode for St. Cecilia's Day, perhaps the last effort of his poetry, has been always considered as exhibiting the highest flight of fancy, and the exactest nicety of art. This is allowed to stand without a rival... Compared with the Ode on Killigrew, it may be pronounced perhaps superior in the whole; but without any single part equal to the first **stanza** of the other."

While considering Dryden a pioneering and refining poet, Johnson was still perceptive enough to see basic weaknesses in Dryden's choice of forms for certain purposes. Johnson felt that "Dryden was no rigid judge of his own pages; he seldom struggled after supreme excellence, but snatched in haste what was within his reach; and when he could content others, was himself contented." At the same time, however, Johnson recognized Dryden's greatness; in the end of "The Life of Dryden," Johnson said that we owed to Dryden "the improvement, perhaps the completion of our metre, the refinement of our language, and much of the correctness of our sentiments." Johnson's final utterance seems perfect; Dryden's effect upon English poetry can be summarized in the Latin expression, lateritiam invenit, marmoream reliquit - "He found it brick, and he left it marble."

LORD MACAULAY

Lord Macaulay (Thomas Babington Macaulay, 1800-1859) was one of the most energetic and respected critics and men of letters in the early nineteenth century. His career began with his 1825 essay on Milton; this was followed in 1828 with an essay on John Dryden. Lord Macaulay opened with an often-quoted statement: "The public voice has assigned to Dryden the first place in the second rank of our poets - no mean station in a table of intellectual precedency so rich in illustrious names."

Macaulay attributes part of Dryden's success to his recognition of the greatness of Milton. (Macaulay notes that Milton was neglected by most of his contemporaries because he surpassed them.) Dryden was not swept up in the stream of bad literature catering to a new public, vulgar taste: "Amidst the crowd of authors who, during the earlier years of Charles the Second, courted notoriety by every species of absurdity and affectation, he speedily became conspicuous. No man exercised so much influence on the age. The reason is obvious. On no man did the age exert so much influence." Macaulay was able to see the important pattern of improvement in Dryden's career as a poet: "His imagination was torpid, till it was awakened by his judgment. He began with quaint parallels and empty mouthing. He gradually acquired the energy of the satirist, the gravity of the moralist, the rapture of the lyric poet. The revolution through which English literature has been passing, from the time of Cowley to that of Scott, may be seen in miniature within the compass of his volumes."

Lord Macaulay never delves very far into the faults and merits of particular poems; he disposes of *Annus Mirabilis*, for example, by merely writing, "The *Annus Mirabilis* shows great command of expression, and a fine ear for heroic **rhyme**. Here its merits end." He even declares almost viciously: "not only has it no claim to be called poetry, but it seems to be the work of a man who could never, by any possibility, write poetry." Dryden's smartest decision was to turn from writing drama to writing poems, particularly the great odes. Macaulay's explanation of Dryden's change is itself almost poetry: "Some years before his death, Dryden altogether ceased to write for the stage. He had turned his powers in a new direction, with success the most splendid and decisive. His taste had gradually awakened his creative faculties... His imagination resembled the wings of an ostrich. It enabled him to run, though not soar. When he attempted the higher flights, he became ridiculous; but, while he remained in a lower region, he outstripped all competitors." Again and again, Macaulay's position is restated: Dryden was a good poet - for the kind of poet he was trying to be, and that was in the second rank of poets.

T. S. ELIOT

When Mark Van Doren published his widely read book on Dryden, T. S. Eliot joined in the praise of a poet who had until recently been only scantily read. Eliot considered Dryden to be a "successor of Jonson, and therefore the descendant of Marlowe; he is the ancestor of nearly all that is best in the poetry of the eighteenth century." This was of course "placing" Dryden in different company from that in which he is placed by Lord Macaulay.

Eliot crystallized one problem we have when assessing Dryden's poetry: most of us have only read - or retained a familiarity with - the satires, with all of their particularity and reference to Dryden's contemporaries; thus Dryden seems "lowered" by nature of his chosen subjects. As Eliot writes,

"Everyone knows *Mac Flecknoe*, and parts of *Absalom and Achitophel*; in consequence, Dryden has sunk by the persons he has elevated to distinction - Shadwell and Settle, Shaftesbury and Buckingham. Dryden was much more than a satirist; to dispose of him as a satirist is to place an obstacle in the way of our understanding."

After thus explaining how we all know *Mac Flecknoe* best, Eliot almost immediately argues that it is, after all, the most entertaining of all of Dryden's poems: "The piece of Dryden's which is the most fun, which is the most sustained display of surprise after surprise of wit from line to line, is *Mac Flecknoe*. Dryden's method here is something very near to **parody**; he applies vocabulary, images, and ceremony which arouse **epic** associations of grandeur, to make an enemy helplessly ridiculous."

Eliot was concerned with understanding why, by way of "taste," we are not particularly attracted to Dryden. He decides that our taste in English poetry has been governed by our recognition of high poetic value in Milton and Shakespeare; our various hopes for poetry are generally achieved in their poetry. By contrast, we do not feel as satisfied when reading through Dryden's poems. Our neglect of Dryden, he says, "is not due to the fact that his work is not poetry, but to a prejudice that the material, the feelings, out of which he built is not poetic." Eliot then gains backing by quoting Matthew Arnold's comment on Dryden and Pope that "their poetry is conceived and composed in their wits, genuine poetry is conceived in the soul."

ELIOT'S LAST WORD

Eliot's final pronouncement on Dryden is deservedly famous; he finds in Dryden a greater statement than suggestiveness (and on this note, we can conclude). "For Dryden, with all his intellect, had a commonplace mind. His powers were, we believe, wider, but no greater, than Milton's; he was confined by boundaries as impassable, though less strait. He bears a curious antithetical resemblance to Swinburne. Swinburne was also a master of words, but Swinburne's words are all suggestions and no **denotation**; if they suggest nothing, it is because they suggest too much. Dryden's words, on the other hand, are precise, they state immensely, but their suggestiveness is often nothing." But Eliot also knew that Dryden's lack of suggestiveness was more than compensated for by his great skill as a versifier; as he writes of Dryden's **elegy** upon Oldham: "From the perfection of such an **elegy** we cannot detract; the lack of suggestiveness is compensated for by the satisfying completeness of the statement. Dryden lacked what his master Jonson possessed: a large and unique view of life; he lacked insight, he lacked profundity (but) he remains one of those who have set standards for English verse which it is desperate to ignore."

BIBLIOGRAPHY

TEXTS

Bredvold, Louis I. (ed.) *The Best of Dryden.* New York, 1933.

Frost, William (ed.) *Selected Works of John Dryden.* New York, 1953. (An extremely useful edition of Dryden's poems, including as well the "verse translations," the *Essay of Dramatic Poetry*, and the Preface to the *Fables.* Frost's commentary on the poems is extremely helpful, particularly to the student approaching Dryden for the first time.)

Gardner, W. Bradford (ed.) *Dryden's Prologues and Epilogues: A Critical Edition.* New York, 1951. (Many of Dryden's better prologues and epilogues are selected carefully for inclusion in Frost's edition.)

Ker, W. P. *Essays of John Dryden.* Oxford, 1900.

Noyes, George R. (ed.) *The Poetical Works of Dryden.* Boston, Rev. edition, 1950. (The best edition of Dryden's poetry, containing extensive notes. Noyes' edition has been of great help in preparing this review book and is invaluable to all serious students of Dryden's poetry.)

Scott, Sir Walter, and Saintsbury, George (eds.) *The Works of John Dryden.* London, 1882-1893. (Many of Scott's interesting and informative comments are included in the notes of the Noyes edition.)

Watson, George (ed.) Dryden. *Of Dramatic Poetry and Other Critical Essays*, 2 Vol. London, 1962. (A good collection of Dryden's critical prose.)

BACKGROUND OF THE AGE

Baugh et al. *A Literary History of* England. New York, 1948.

Beljame, Alexandre. Men of Letters and the English Public in the Eighteenth-Century, 1660-1744; trans. by E. O. Lorimer, London, 1948.

Borgman, A. S. Thomas Shadwell. New York, 1958.

Bredvold, Louis I. The Intellectual Milieu of John Dryden: Studies in Some Aspects of Seventeenth-Century Thought. Ann Arbor, 1937. (Bredvold's book has become something of a minor classic. It is virtually indispensable when coming to grips with the intellectual aspect of Dryden. It is a judicious and valuable critical work.)

Brownowski, J. and Mazlish, B. The Western Intellectual Tradition. New York, 1960 (Historians look carefully at the men and the customs of the Restoration.)

Bush, Douglas. English Poetry. New York, 1963.

Ford, Boris (ed.) From Dryden to Johnson (Vol. IV of the Pelican Guide to English Literature) Baltimore, 1957.

Grierson, H. J. C. Cross-Currents in English Literature of the XVIIth Century. London, 1929.

Wedgwood, C. V. Seventeenth-Century English Literature. New York, 1961.

Wiley, Basil. The Seventeenth Century Background. London, 1939.

BIOGRAPHY OF DRYDEN

Johnson, Samuel. "Life of Dryden" in *The Lives of the Poets*. (Many editions. Johnson's Life of Dryden is entertaining and judicious; for some of Johnson's views, see the Critical Commentary.)

Noyes, G. R. "Biographical Sketch" in *Poetical Works of Dryden*. (Considered by Frost and others to be the best account.)

Osborn, James M. *John Dryden: Some Biographical Facts and Problems*. New York, 1940. (This reviews the earlier biographies.)

Scott, Sir Walter. "Life of Dryden," *Works of John Dryden*, cit.

Untermeyer, Louis. *Lives of the Poets*. New York, 1959. (Very readable and a quick way to familiarize oneself with the main points.)

Ward, Charles E. *The Life of John Dryden*, 1961.

_____ *The Letters of John Dryden*. Durham, N. C., 1942.

Young, Kenneth. *John Dryden; A Critical Biography*. London, 1954.

CRITICISM

Amarasinghe, Upali. *Dryden and Pope In the Early Nineteenth Century*. Cambridge, 1962.

Brennecke, Ernest H. Jr. "Dryden's Odes and Draghi's Music," *Publication of the Modern Language Association*, XLIX (1934).

Daiches, David. *A Critical History of English Literature*, Vol. II. New York, 1960. (Contains a good survey of the age of the Restoration, in addition to discussion of particular Dryden poems.)

Eliot, T. S. *Homage to John Dryden: Three Essays on the Poetry of the Seventeenth Century.* London, 1924.

_____ *Selected Essays of T. S. Eliot.* New York, 1932.

_____ John Dryden: The Poet, The Dramatist, the Critic. *New York, 1932.*

Frost, William. *Dryden and the Art of Translation.* New Haven, 1955.

Hoffman, Arthur W. *John Dryden's **Imagery**.* Gainesville, Florida, 1962.

Hollander, John. *The Untuning of the Sky.* Princeton, 1961.

Kinsley, James. "Dryden and the Encomium Musicae," *Review of English Studies*, New Series. IV (1952).

Macaulay, Lord. Critical, Historical, and Miscellaneous Essays. *Vol I, New York, 1880.*

Schilling, Bernard N. (ed.) Dryden. *A Collection Of Critical Essays.* Englewood Cliffs, 1963. (An excellent collection, including essays by such eminent Dryden critics as James Osborn, E. M. W. Tillyard, John Hollander, and Edwin Morgan. One should read Reuben A. Brower's well-known essay, "An **Allusion** to Europe: Dryden and Poetic Tradition," originally included in Professor Brower's *Alexander Pope: The Poetry of **Allusion**.* Oxford, 1959.)

_____ Dryden and the Conservative Myth; A Reading of Absalom and Achitophel. *New Haven, 1961.*

Sharp, R. L. *From Donne to Dryden. The Revolt Against Metaphysical Poetry.* North Carolina, 1940.

Sutherland, James. *John Dryden. The Poet as Orator.* W. P. Ker memorial lecture, Glasgow, 1963. (An interesting account of oratorical tradition and style in Dryden's poetry.)

Van Doren, Mark. *John Dryden: A Study of His Poetry.* New York, 1920; rev. ed., 1946. (A well-known minor classic in Dryden criticism.)

Verrall, A. W. *Lectures on Dryden.* Cambridge, 1914.

Wallenstein, Ruth C. "The Development of the Rhetoric and Metre of the Heroic **Couplet**, Especially in 1625-1645." *Publication of The Modern Language Association*, L (1935).

Williamson, George. "The Rhetorical Pattern of Neo-classical Wit," *Modern Philology*, XXVIII (1935).

FURTHER BIBLIOGRAPHIES

Macdonald, Hugh. *John Dryden: A Bibliography of Early Editions and of Drydeniana.* New York, 1939.

Monk, Samuel H. *John Dryden: A List of Critical Studies Published from 1895 to 1948.* Minneapolis, 1950.

www.ingramcontent.com/pod-product-compliance
Lightning Source LLC
LaVergne TN
LVHW012057070526
838200LV00070BA/2786